MODERN-DAY BIRD CHALLENGES IN INDIA

Mr. MRIDUL LAMBA

PhD Scholar, Department of Zoology,
School of Basic and Applied Sciences, Raffles University,
Neemrana - 301705, Alwar, Rajasthan, India.

Mrs. SAPNA REDHU

PhD Scholar, Department of Biotechnology,
Chaudhary Devi Lal University, Sirsa - 125055, Haryana, India.

DR. NAVEEN KUMAR

Assistant Professor, Department of Zoology,
School of Basic and Applied Sciences, Raffles University,
Neemrana - 301705, Alwar, Rajasthan, India.

Title : Modern-Day Bird Challenges in India

Author : Mr. Mridul Lamba, Mrs. Sapna Redhu, Dr. Naveen Kumar

Edition : First (Septermber, 2024)

ISBN : 9788197785702

Published by

 **PRACHI**
DIGITAL PUBLICATION

Regd. Add.: 254, Khuriyakhatta No. 10, Bindukhatta, Lalkuan, Nainital - 262402, Uttarakhand, India

Website : www.prachidigital.com

E-mail : info@prachidigital.in

Phone : +91 976041 7980, +91 976041 8103

Printed by :

Manipal Technologies Limited, Bengaluru - 560001, Karnataka

PREFACE

The intricate tapestry of India's avian diversity is a testament to the country's rich natural heritage. From the snow-capped peaks of the Himalayas to the sun-drenched coasts of the southern peninsula, India's landscapes are alive with the vibrant colors and songs of over 1,350 bird species. These feathered inhabitants play vital roles in maintaining ecological balance, acting as pollinators, seed dispersers, pest controllers, and indicators of environmental health. However, this avian splendor faces unprecedented challenges that threaten to unravel the delicate ecological fabric. This book, **"Modern-Day Bird Challenges in India,"** is a comprehensive exploration of the myriad threats confronting India's bird populations. Authored by dedicated researchers and scholars deeply immersed in the study of avian ecology, the chapters meticulously examine the diverse habitats birds inhabit, the ecological roles they play, and the dire consequences of habitat loss, pollution, climate change, poaching, and human-wildlife conflicts.

The motivation for this book arose from an urgent need to highlight the plight of birds amidst India's rapid urbanization and industrialization. Through rigorous research and field studies, we aim to shed light on the critical issues facing these winged sentinels of our environment. Each chapter delves into specific challenges, offering insights into habitat degradation, the impact of pollutants, the perils of illegal trade, and the intricate dynamics of human-bird interactions.

We also celebrate the remarkable resilience and adaptability of birds, showcasing their unique adaptations to India's diverse environments. From the majestic Indian Peafowl, our national bird, to the elusive Great Indian Bustard, each species' story underscores the urgent need for conservation efforts. The book also emphasizes the significance of community involvement, sustainable practices, and policy interventions in safeguarding our avian heritage.

Our hope is that this book serves as a clarion call to policymakers, conservationists, and the general public to recognize and act upon the pressing challenges facing India's birds. By understanding the complex web of factors threatening these species, we can better appreciate the necessity of conserving their habitats and ensuring their survival for future generations.

As you journey through the pages of this book, we invite you to reflect on the beauty and fragility of India's avian diversity. Let this be a source of inspiration to contribute to the ongoing efforts to protect and preserve the incredible birdlife that enriches our landscapes and our lives.

Ms. Mridul Lamba
Mrs. Sapna Redhu
Dr. Naveen Kumar

ABOUT THE BOOK

"Modern-Day Bird Challenges in India" is an in-depth examination of the multifaceted threats facing India's diverse avian population. Written by leading researchers and scholars in the field of ornithology, this book provides a thorough analysis of the current state of bird species across the country, highlighting the critical issues and proposing viable solutions for conservation.

The book is divided into several comprehensive chapters, each addressing a specific aspect of avian ecology and the challenges that come with it. From habitat loss and degradation due to urbanization and deforestation to the impacts of pollution, climate change, and human-wildlife conflicts, the authors present a detailed account of the factors contributing to the decline in bird populations. Additionally, the book explores the illegal trade and poaching of birds, collisions with infrastructure, and the complexities of managing human-bird interactions in both urban and rural settings.

Data Sheets

The data sheets included in book provide a comprehensive compilation of critical information on bird species, their conservation status, and the myriad challenges they face. These data sheets cover various aspects such as the conservation status and diversity of bird species in India, trends in bird populations, the impact of habitat loss and degradation, pollution threats, climate change effects, and the consequences of poaching and illegal trade. Additionally, they address the impact of infrastructure development, human-wildlife conflict, and biomagnification on avian species. By offering detailed statistics, trends, and case studies, these data sheets serve as an invaluable resource for researchers, policymakers, conservationists, and educators, enabling them to make informed decisions and implement effective conservation strategies.

Based on these studies, various aspects of the chapters have been formed, providing a solid foundation for the detailed discussions and analyses presented throughout the book. The data sheets underscore the urgency of conservation efforts and highlight successful initiatives, providing a solid foundation for future actions aimed at protecting India's rich avian biodiversity.

CHAPTER SUMMARIES

Chapter 1: A Celebration of India's Avian Riches

This chapter highlights the incredible diversity of bird species in India, exploring their various habitats, behaviors, and adaptations. It sets the stage for understanding the importance of birds in India's ecosystems and introduces readers to the country's most iconic avian species.

Chapter 2: The Looming Crisis: Challenges Faced by India's Birds

An overview of the major threats facing bird populations in India, including habitat loss, pollution, climate change, poaching, and human-wildlife conflicts. This chapter provides a broad context for the more detailed discussions that follow.

Chapter 3: Habitat Loss and Degradation: A Deeper Dive

Delving into the specifics of how urbanization, agriculture, and deforestation are shrinking and fragmenting bird habitats, this chapter examines the consequences of habitat loss on bird populations and the ecosystem services they provide.

Chapter 4: Pollution's Peril: A Multifaceted Threat

This chapter addresses the various forms of pollution—air, water, and electromagnetic—that affect birds. It explores how industrial effluents, agricultural runoff, and urban emissions contribute to the decline in bird health and populations.

Chapter 5: Climate Change: Altered Ecosystems Impact on Avian Survival

The impacts of climate change on birds are profound and multifaceted. This chapter discusses how rising temperatures, shifting rainfall patterns, and extreme weather events are disrupting bird habitats, migration routes, and breeding cycles.

Chapter 6: Poaching and Illegal Trade: The Willful Damage

Focusing on the illegal capture and trade of birds, this chapter highlights the species most at risk and the conservation efforts needed to combat poaching and illegal trade.

Chapter 7: Collisions with Infrastructure: Urban Development Hazards

Urban development presents new hazards for birds, from collisions with buildings to deaths caused by power lines and wind turbines. This chapter explores these threats and discusses ways to design bird-friendly infrastructure.

Chapter 8: Human-Wildlife Conflict: Sharing Space Sharing Challenges

Birds and humans often come into conflict, especially in agricultural and urban settings. This chapter examines the causes of these conflicts and offers strategies for fostering coexistence.

"Modern-Day Bird Challenges in India" is not only a scientific treatise but also a call to action. It seeks to engage policymakers, conservationists, and the general public, urging them to take immediate and sustained action to address the urgent threats facing India's birds. The authors provide practical recommendations for habitat restoration, pollution control, climate change mitigation, and the enforcement of anti-poaching laws.

This book serves as an essential resource for anyone interested in the conservation of birds and biodiversity in India. It combines rigorous scientific research with compelling narratives and vivid illustrations, making it accessible to a broad audience, from students and academics to nature enthusiasts and policymakers.

By reading this book, you will gain a deeper understanding of the ecological, cultural, and economic significance of birds in India. It aims to inspire a collective effort to protect these incredible creatures and the natural habitats they depend on, ensuring their survival for generations to come.

TABLE OF CONTENTS

Chapter 1: A Celebration of India's Avian Riches

1. The Symphony of Feathers
2. A Land of Soaring Beauty
3. India's Diverse Avian Realms
4. India's Feathered Icons
5. Avian Adaptations: Thriving in Diverse Environments

Chapter 2: The Looming Crisis: Challenges Faced by India's Birds

1. Habitat Loss and Degradation: A Shrinking Sanctuary
2. The Shadow of Pollution: A Toxic Threat to Avian Health
3. Climate Change: A Shifting Landscape
4. The Peril of Exploitation: Poaching, Illegal Trade, and Collisions
5. Human-Wildlife Conflict: Sharing Space with Challenges

Chapter 3: Habitat Loss and Degradation: A Deeper Dive

1. A Symphony of Ecosystems: Understanding Bird Habitats in India
2. The Price of Progress: Analyzing Habitat Loss and its Consequences
3. Consequences of Fragmentation: Isolating Bird Populations
4. Habitat Restoration: Efforts to Reclaim Lost Paradise
5. Citizen Science: Monitoring Bird Populations and Habitat Health

Chapter 4: Pollution's Peril: A Multifaceted Threat

1. A Toxic Cocktail: Sources and Impacts of Pollution on Birds
2. Beyond the Obvious: Exploring Air and Electromagnetic Pollution
3. Water Pollution's Devastating Impact
4. The Effects of Light Pollution

Chapter 5: Climate Change: Altered Ecosystems Impact on Avian Survival

1. Rising Temperatures: A Feverish Threat to Bird Habitats
2. Shifting Distribution Ranges: A Scramble for Survival
3. The Plight of Migratory Birds: Facing Double Jeopardy
4. The Domino Effect: Climate Change and Cascading Impacts.
5. Adaptation and Conservation: Strategies for a Changing Climate

Chapter 6: Poaching and Illegal Trade: The Wilful Damage

1. Defying Legal Protections: The Persistence of Poaching
2. A Multi-Billion Dollar Crime: The Illegal Wildlife Trade
3. The Human Cost of Poaching and Illegal Trade
4. Combating the Illegal Trade: Law Enforcement and Conservation Efforts
5. A Sustainable Future: Balancing Conservation and Livelihoods

Chapter 7: Collisions with Infrastructure: Urban Development Hazards

1. A Modern Threat: Birds and Man-Made Structures
2. Urban Environments: A Labyrinth of Risks
3. Case Studies: Avian Casualties and the Need for Solutions

4. Finding Solutions: Bird-Friendly Infrastructure Design
5. Public Awareness and Citizen Science
Chapter 8: Human-Wildlife Conflict: Sharing Space, Sharing Challenges
1. Crop Raiding and Property Damage: Understanding Bird Behavior
2. Retaliatory Killings and Habitat Destruction: A Vicious Cycle
3. Case Studies: Human-Bird Conflicts in India
4. Beyond Coexistence: Fostering Positive Human-Bird Relationships
5. Finding Solutions: Strategies for Effective Human-Wildlife Conflict Management
References

DATA SHEETS

DATA SHEET - I	Conservation Status and Bird Species Diversity in India (The IUCN Red List of India)
DATA SHEET - II	Trends and Challenges in India's Bird Populations
DATA SHEET - III	Impact of Habitat Loss on Avian Species in India
DATA SHEET - IV	Pollution's Peril: A Multifaceted Threat to Birds
DATA SHEET - V	Impact of Climate Change on Avian Species in India
DATA SHEET - VI	Impact of Poaching and Illegal Trade on Avian Species in India
DATA SHEET - VII	Impact of Infrastructure development on Avian Species in India
DATA SHEET - VIII	Impact of Human-Wildlife Conflict on Avian Species in India

DATA SHEET - I

CONSERVATION STATUS AND BIRD SPECIES DIVERSITY IN INDIA

The IUCN Red List [1]

Bird Species in India

India is home to approximately 1,350 bird species, which accounts for about 12% of the world's bird species. This diversity includes both resident and migratory birds that use India as a seasonal refuge.

Conservation Status of Birds in India

The conservation status of bird species in India varies widely. According to the 2023 State of India's Birds report, birds in India have been classified into different categories based on their risk of extinction, as assessed by the International Union for Conservation of Nature (IUCN).

The IUCN Red List categorizes 182 species of Indian birds as Critically Endangered, Endangered, Vulnerable, and Near Threatened, indicating their threat of global extinction. International trade in these species is banned, reflecting their special significance as endemic to the Indian Subcontinent and highlighting the critical need for their conservation.

The categories are as follows:

Critically Endangered: 17 species

Endangered: 21 species

Vulnerable: 63 species

Near Threatened: 81 species

Least Concern: The majority of the remaining species

CRITICALLY ENDANGERED

1. Baer's Pochard – (*Aythya baeri*)
2. Bengal Florican – (*Houbaropsis bengalensis*)
3. Bugun Liocichla – (*Liocichla bugunorum*)
4. Christmas Island Frigatebird – (*Fregata andrewsi*)
5. Great Indian Bustard – (*Ardeotis nigriceps*)
6. Himalayan Quail – (*Ophrysia superciliosa*)
7. Indian Vulture – (*Gyps indicus*)
8. Jerdon's Courser – (*Rhinoptilus bitorquatus*)
9. Pink-headed Duck – (*Rhodonessa caryophyllacea*)
10. Red-headed Vulture – (*Sarcogyps calvus*)
11. Siberian Crane – (*Leucogeranus leucogeranus*)
12. Slender-billed Vulture – (*Gyps tenuirostris*)
13. Sociable Lapwing – (*Vanellus gregarious*)
14. Spoon-billed Sandpiper - *Calidris pygmaea*
15. White-bellied Heron - *Ardea insignis*
16. White-rumped Vulture - *Gyps bengalensis*
17. Yellow-breasted Bunting - *Emberiza aureola*

ENDANGERED

1. Banasura Laughingthrush - *Montecincla jerdoni*
2. Barau's Petrel - *Pterodroma baraui*
3. Black-bellied Tern - *Sterna acuticauda*
4. Egyptian Vulture - *Neophron percnopterus*
5. Forest Owlet - *Athene blewitti*
6. Great Knot - *Calidris tenuirostris*
7. Greater Adjutant - *Leptoptilos dubius*
8. Green Peafowl - *Pavo muticus*
9. Lesser Florican - *Sypheotides indicus*
10. Manipur Bush-quail - *Perdicula manipurensis*
11. Masked Finfoot - *Heliopais personatus*
12. Narcondam Hornbill - *Rhyticeros narcondami*
13. Nilgiri Blue Robin - *Sholicola major*
14. Nilgiri Laughingthrush - *Montecincla cachinnans*
15. Pallas's Fish-eagle - *Haliaeetus leucoryphus*
16. Saker Falcon - *Falco cherrug*
17. Steppe Eagle - *Aquila nipalensis*
18. Swamp Grass-babbler - *Laticilla cinerascens*
19. White-eared Night-heron - *Gorsachius magnificus*
20. White-headed Duck - *Oxyura leucocephala*
21. White-winged Wood Duck - *Asarcornis scutulata*

VULNERABLE

1. Andaman Serpent-eagle - *Spilornis elgini*
2. Andaman Teal - *Anas albogularis*
3. Andaman Treepie - *Dendrocitta bayleii*
4. Andaman Woodpecker - *Dryocopus hodgei*
5. Beautiful Nuthatch - *Sitta formosa*
6. Black-breasted Parrotbill - *Paradoxornis flavirostris*
7. Black-legged Kittiwake - *Rissa tridactyla*
8. Black-necked Crane - *Grus nigricollis*
9. Blyth's Tragopan - *Tragopan blythii*
10. Bristled Grassbird - *Schoenicola striatus*
11. Broad-tailed Grassbird - *Schoenicola platyurus*
12. Cheer Pheasant - *Catreus wallichii*
13. Chestnut-breasted Partridge - *Arborophila mandellii*
14. Chinese Egret - *Egretta eulophotes*
15. Common Pochard - *Aythya ferina*
16. Dark-rumped Swift - *Apus acuticauda*
17. Eastern Imperial Eagle - *Aquila heliaca*
18. European Turtle-dove - *Streptopelia turtur*
19. Finn's Weaver - *Ploceus megarhynchus*
20. Great Hornbill - *Buceros bicornis*
21. Great Slaty Woodpecker - *Mulleripicus pulverulentus*
22. Greater Spotted Eagle - *Clanga clanga*
23. Green Avadavat - *Amandava formosa*
24. Grey-crowned Prinia - *Prinia cinereocapilla*
25. Grey-sided Thrush - *Turdus feae*
26. Horned Grebe - *Podiceps auritus*
27. Indian Skimmer - *Rynchops albicollis*
28. Indian Spotted Eagle - *Clanga hastata*
29. Jerdon's Babbler - *Chrysomma altirostre*
30. Kashmir Flycatcher - *Ficedula subrubra*
31. Lesser Adjutant - *Leptoptilos javanicus*
32. Lesser White-fronted Goose - *Anser erythropus*
33. Long-tailed Duck - *Clangula hyemalis*
34. Long-tailed Parakeet - *Psittacula longicauda*
35. Macqueen's Bustard - *Chlamydotis macqueenii*
36. Marbled Teal - *Marmaronetta angustirostris*
37. Marsh Babbler - *Pellorneum palustre*
38. Nicobar Megapode - *Megapodius nicobariensis*
39. Nicobar Sparrowhawk - *Accipiter butleri*
40. Nilgiri Pipit - *Anthus nilghiriensis*
41. Nilgiri Wood Pigeon - *Columba elphinstonii*

42. Pale-capped Pigeon - *Columba punicea*
43. Red-breasted Goose - *Branta ruficollis*
44. Rufous-necked Hornbill - *Aceros nipalensis*
45. Rusty-throated Wren-babbler - *Spelaeornis badeigularis*
46. Sarus Crane - *Antigone antigone*
47. Sclater's Monal - *Lophophorus sclateri*
48. Slender-billed Babbler - *Argya longirostris*
49. Snowy-throated Babbler - *Stachyris oglei*
50. Swamp Francolin - *Francolinus gularis*
51. Tawny Eagle - *Aquila rapax*
52. Tawny-breasted Wren-babbler - *Spelaeornis longicaudatus*
53. Travancore Laughingthrush - *Trochalopteron meridionale*
54. Western Tragopan - *Tragopan melanocephalus*
55. White-bellied Blue Robin - *Sholicola albiventris*
56. White-browed Bush Chat - *Saxicola macrorhynchus*
57. White-naped Tit - *Machlolophus nuchalis*
58. White-throated Bush Chat - *Saxicola insignis*
59. Wood Snipe - *Gallinago nemoricola*
60. Woolly-necked Stork- *Ciconia episcopus*
61. Wreathed Hornbill - *Rhyticeros undulatus*
62. Yellow-eyed Pigeon - *Columba eversmanni*
63. Yellow-throated Bulbul - *Pycnonotus xantholaemus*

NEAR THREATENED
1. Alexandrine Parakeet - *Psittacula eupatria*
2. Andaman Cuckooshrike - *Coracina dobsoni*
3. Andaman Green-pigeon - *Treron chloropterus*
4. Andaman Woodpigeon - *Columba palumboides*
5. Ashy-headed Green-pigeon - *Treron phayrei*
6. Asian Dowitcher - *Limnodromus semipalmatus*
7. Austen's Brown Hornbill - *Anorrhinus austeni*
8. Bar-tailed Godwit - *Limosa lapponica*
9. Beach Stone-Curlew - *Esacus magnirostris*
10. Bearded Vulture - *Gypaetus barbatus*
11. Black-headed Ibis - *Threskiornis melanocephalus*
12. Blackish-breasted Babbler - *Stachyris humei*
13. Black-necked Stork - *Ephippiorhynchus asiaticus*
14. Black-tailed Godwit - *Limosa limosa*
15. Blossom-headed Parakeet - *Psittacula roseata*
16. Blyth's Kingfisher - *Alcedo hercules*
17. Brown-winged Kingfisher - *Pelargopsis amauroptera*
18. Buff-breasted Sandpiper - *Calidris subruficollis*
19. Chestnut-backed Laughingthrush - *Pterorhinus nuchalis*

20. Chevron-breasted Babbler - *Stachyris roberti*
21. Cinereous Vulture - *Aegypius monachus*
22. Curlew Sandpiper - *Calidris ferruginea*
23. Dalmatian Pelican - *Pelecanus crispus*
24. Eurasian Curlew - *Numenius arquata*
25. Eurasian Oystercatcher - *Haematopus ostralegus*
26. Falcated Duck - *Mareca falcata*
27. Ferruginous Duck - *Aythya nyroca*
28. Firethroat - *Calliope pectardens*
29. Flesh-footed Shearwater - *Ardenna carneipes*
30. Great Nicobar Serpent-eagle - *Spilornis klossi*
31. Great Snipe - *Gallinago media*
32. Great Stone-Curlew - *Esacus recurvirostris*
33. Grey-headed Bulbul - *Pycnonotus priocephalus*
34. Grey-headed Fish-eagle - *Icthyophaga ichthyaetus*
35. Grey-headed Parakeet - *Psittacula finschii*
36. Grey-tailed Tattler - *Tringa brevipes*
37. Himalayan Griffon - *Gyps himalayensis*
38. Indian Grassbird - *Graminicola bengalensis*
39. Japanese Quail - *Coturnix japonica*
40. Jouanin's Petrel - *Bulweria fallax*
41. Laggar Falcon - *Falco jugger*
42. Lesser Fish-eagle - *Icthyophaga humilis*
43. Lesser Flamingo - *Phoeniconaias minor*
44. Little Bustard - Tetrax *tetrax*
45. Long-billed Bush-warbler - *Locustella major*
46. Lord Derby's Parakeet - *Psittacula derbiana*
47. Malabar Pied Hornbill - *Anthracoceros coronatus*
48. Mangrove Pitta - *Pitta megarhyncha*
49. Mrs Hume's Pheasant - *Syrmaticus humiae*
50. Naga Wren-babbler - *Spelaeornis chocolatinus*
51. Nicobar Bulbul - *Ixos nicobariensis*
52. Nicobar Jungle Flycatcher - *Cyornis nicobaricus*
53. Nicobar Parakeet - *Psittacula caniceps*
54. Nicobar Pigeon - *Caloenas nicobarica*
55. Nicobar Scops-owl - *Otus alius*
56. Northern Lapwing - *Vanellus vanellus*
57. Oriental Darter - *Anhinga melanogaster*
58. Painted Stork - *Mycteria leucocephala*
59. Palani Laughingthrush - *Montecincla fairbanki*
60. Pallid Harrier - *Circus macrourus*
61. Red Kite - *Milvus milvus*

62. Red Knot - *Calidris canutus*
63. Red-breasted Parakeet - *Psittacula alexandri*
64. Red-footed Falcon - *Falco vespertinus*
65. Red-necked Falcon - *Falco chicquera*
66. Red-necked Stint - *Calidris ruficollis*
67. River Lapwing - *Vanellus duvaucelii*
68. River Tern - *Sterna aurantia*
69. Rufous-bellied Eagle - *Lophotriorchis kienerii*
70. Rufous-throated Wren babbler - *Spelaeornis caudatus*
71. Rufous-vented Grass-babbler - *Laticilla burnesii*
72. Rusty-bellied Shortwing - *Brachypteryx hyperythra*
73. Satyr Tragopan - *Tragopan satyra*
74. Spot-billed Pelican - *Pelecanus philippensis*
75. Streaked Shearwater - *Calonectris leucomelas*
76. Swinhoe's Storm-petrel - *Oceanodroma monorhis*
77. Tytler's Leaf warbler - *Phylloscopus tytleri*
78. Ward's Trogon - *Harpactes wardi*
79. White-cheeked Hill Partridge - *Arborophila atrogularis*
80. Yellow-rumped Honeyguide - *Indicator xanthonotus*
81. Yunnan Nuthatch - *Sitta yunnanensis*

Trends in Bird Diversity

The State of India's Birds report of 2023 highlights significant trends in bird populations across India. Over the past 25 years, many bird species have shown alarming declines. The key findings include:

Grassland Birds: Populations of grassland birds have declined by more than 50% due to habitat loss and degradation.

Migratory Shorebirds: These birds, which breed in the Arctic and migrate to India's coastal habitats, have declined by nearly 80%.

Raptors: Species such as the Pallas's Fish Eagle have seen rapid declines due to habitat destruction and pollution.

Resident Species: While many migratory species are in decline, some resident species like the Indian Peafowl and Asian Koel have shown population stability or growth, adapting well to changing environments and urban settings.

CHAPTER 1

A Celebration of India's Avian Riches

1. The Symphony of Feathers
1.1 Global Chorus: Exploring Global Bird Diversity

Birds are among the most captivating creatures, showcasing a remarkable diversity across continents and oceans. They inhabit nearly every conceivable environment, from the icy Arctic to the dense Amazon rainforests, and from arid deserts to the open skies above oceans. This adaptability underscores their evolutionary success, with over 10,000 recognized species each uniquely adapted to their ecological niches. The vast spectrum of bird species is a product of millions of years of evolution, shaped by natural selection and environmental pressures. From the tiny bee hummingbird, measuring just 5 cm, to the towering ostrich, standing at over 2.7 meters, birds exhibit profound variations in size, form, and color. Their evolutionary history is deeply intertwined with our planet's history, descending from theropod dinosaurs and evolving features such as feathers, beaks, and flight capabilities.

Birds play crucial roles in ecosystems worldwide. They serve as pollinators, seed dispersers, predators, and prey, contributing significantly to the balance of nature. Hummingbirds, sunbirds, and honeyeaters are vital pollinators, while birds like Clark's nutcracker and the New Zealand kiwi aid in forest regeneration by dispersing seeds. Raptors such as eagles and hawks maintain ecological equilibrium by preying on small mammals and other birds. The migratory patterns of birds are among nature's most awe-inspiring phenomena. Millions of birds undertake long, perilous journeys between breeding and wintering grounds annually. The Arctic tern, for instance, travels a round trip of about 40,000 kilometers from the Arctic to the Antarctic. These migrations highlight the interconnectedness of global ecosystems and the need for international conservation efforts.

Birdsong, another fascinating aspect of avian diversity, serves multiple purposes, from attracting mates and defending territories to coordinating group activities and warning of predators. The complexity of birdsong varies widely, with species like the nightingale and lyrebird renowned for their elaborate melodies, while the mimic thrush can imitate a range of sounds, including mechanical noises. The conservation of bird diversity is a pressing global issue, with habitat loss, climate change, pollution, and hunting posing significant threats. Many species are endangered or threatened, emphasizing the need for conservation initiatives such as protected areas, habitat restoration, and legal protections. Birds also hold significant cultural and symbolic value, appearing in myths, legends, and art across different cultures, underscoring the importance of their preservation not just for ecological reasons but also for their cultural and aesthetic value.

1.2 Avian Abundance in India: A Rich Tapestry of Species

Globally, there are over 10,000 recognized bird species, each boasting distinct characteristics, behaviors, and habitats, a testament to millions of years of evolution shaped by natural selection and environmental pressures. From the tiny bee hummingbird, at just 5 centimeters, to the towering ostrich, over 2.7 meters tall, birds exhibit a remarkable range of sizes, forms, and plumages, displaying both beauty and camouflage. Birds' evolutionary history intertwines with our planet's past. Descendants of theropod dinosaurs, their evolution showcases life's adaptability. The fossil record reveals their journey, from ancient ancestors to modern avians with feathers, beaks, and flight capabilities. This evolutionary saga reflects not just survival but flourishing in diverse environments.

Ecologically, birds play vital roles. They are pollinators, seed dispersers, predators, and prey, maintaining ecological balance. Hummingbirds, sunbirds, and honeyeaters pollinate plants, while species like Clark's nutcracker and the New Zealand kiwi disperse seeds, aiding forest regeneration. Raptors, such as eagles and hawks, control populations of small mammals and other birds. Bird migration is a remarkable natural phenomenon. Millions embark on perilous journeys between breeding and wintering grounds. The Arctic tern's 40,000-kilometer round trip from the Arctic to the Antarctic exemplifies endurance and the interconnectedness of global ecosystems, underscoring the need for international conservation efforts. Birdsong is another captivating aspect of avian diversity. Unique calls and songs serve multiple purposes: attracting mates, defending territories, coordinating group activities, and warning of predators. Some species, like the nightingale and lyrebird, are renowned for their elaborate songs, while mimics like the thrush can imitate a wide range of sounds.

Morphologically, birds are equally diverse. Beak shapes and sizes are adapted to dietary needs, from the hummingbird's nectar-extracting beak to the eagle's flesh-tearing hook. Feet vary too, with webbed feet for swimming, strong talons for hunting, and perching feet for songbirds. Socially, birds display a variety of structures and reproductive strategies, from solitary to large flocks, monogamous pairs, and cooperative breeding.

2. A Land of Soaring Beauty

2.1 Endemic Gems: India's Unique and Precious Birds

India, a land renowned for its rich biodiversity, hosts a multitude of habitats supporting a vast array of avian species, including many endemics that represent unique ecological niches. These birds are not only vital indicators of environmental health but also cultural treasures, reflecting India's natural heritage. They thrive across diverse landscapes-from the Himalayas and Western Ghats to Rajasthan's deserts and the northeastern wetlands-each uniquely adapted to its environment and contributing to ecological balance and evolutionary insights. The Indian Peafowl (Pavo cristatus), India's national bird, is celebrated for its vibrant plumage and majestic courtship displays. Predominantly found in the subcontinent's deciduous forests and scrublands, its elaborate dances signify the monsoon's onset, symbolizing the deep connections between wildlife and India's seasonal cycles.

In the Western Ghats, the Malabar Grey Hornbill (Ocyceros griseus) plays a crucial role in seed dispersal, aiding forest regeneration. This medium-sized hornbill, a flagship species of the UNESCO World Heritage Site, relies on large trees for nesting and fruit-bearing trees for food, highlighting the interdependence between species and their habitats. The Himalayan Monal (Lophophorus impejanus), with its iridescent plumage, inhabits the rugged terrains of the Himalayas. Adapted to high altitudes, this state bird of Uttarakhand faces threats from human activities, necessitating conservation efforts to ensure its survival amidst the harsh winters.

The critically endangered Great Indian Bustard (Ardeotis nigriceps) stands as a sentinel of Rajasthan's grasslands. Once widespread, it now faces severe threats from habitat loss and hunting. Conservation initiatives focusing on habitat restoration and community involvement are vital for its survival. The recently discovered Bugun Liocichla (Liocichla bugunorum) in Arunachal Pradesh underscores the unexplored biodiversity of India. Found in the dense undergrowth of subtropical forests, its discovery has spurred regional conservation efforts to protect these unique ecosystems.

The Andaman Serpent Eagle (Spilornis elgini) of the Andaman and Nicobar Islands exemplifies endemism in remote archipelagos. This apex predator maintains ecological balance in tropical rainforests and mangroves, emphasizing the need for stringent protection measures against natural disasters and human interference. India's endemic birds, from the Nilgiri Flycatcher (Eumyias albicaudatus) in the Western Ghats to the Indian Skimmer (Rynchops albicollis) along large rivers, illustrate the complexity and fragility of natural ecosystems. Conservation efforts must prioritize habitat protection and restoration, with public awareness and education playing critical roles in fostering a collective movement to preserve India's natural heritage.

2.2 Ecological Indicators: Showcasing Birds as Guardians of Habitats

The house sparrow (Passer domesticus) is a notable example of an ecological indicator in India. Once common in both urban and rural areas, its population decline signals significant environmental shifts. Sparrows reflect urban ecological health, with trends indicating changes in habitat quality, food availability, and pollution levels. Declines are linked to urbanization, pesticide pollution, and modern architectural designs that limit nesting sites. Conservation efforts focus on creating bird-friendly urban spaces, promoting organic farming, and encouraging nesting-friendly architecture. Wetland birds also serve as crucial indicators. Species like the Indian skimmer (Rynchops albicollis) and the black-necked stork (Ephippiorhynchus asiaticus) highlight the health of wetland ecosystems. These birds are sensitive to water quality and availability changes. The Indian skimmer's foraging depends on stable water levels, and its population decline signals wetland health deterioration due to pollution and unregulated development. Conservation involves wetland restoration, pollution control, and sustainable water management.

Forest birds such as the Great Hornbill (Buceros bicornis) and Malabar Trogon (Harpactes fasciatus) are indicators of forest ecosystem health. The Great Hornbill's presence signifies a mature, resource-rich forest, contributing to seed dispersal and regeneration. Their decline reflects habitat destruction and logging. Conservation strategies include safeguarding large forest tracts, combating illegal logging, and promoting sustainable management. Grassland birds, including the critically endangered Great Indian Bustard (Ardeotis nigriceps) and Lesser Florican (Sypheotides indicus), indicate grassland ecosystem health. The Bustard's population, now fewer than 200, highlights habitat degradation due to agricultural expansion and infrastructure development. Conservation focuses on habitat restoration, creating protected areas, and implementing sustainable grazing practices, with community involvement being crucial.

Coastal and marine birds like the Narcondam Hornbill (Rhyticeros narcondami) indicate coastal ecosystem health. These birds are vulnerable to habitat disturbances and invasive species. Conservation involves protecting nesting sites, managing invasive species, and regulating coastal development. Birds in agricultural landscapes, such as the Indian Roller (Coracias benghalensis), indicate agroecosystem health. Declines in their populations suggest overuse of pesticides and habitat loss. Promoting integrated pest management and organic farming can create bird-friendly agricultural landscapes. Birds across various ecosystems-urban, forest, wetland, grassland, coastal, and agricultural-serve as critical indicators of environmental health. Their populations and behaviors provide valuable insights, guiding conservation efforts to preserve biodiversity and ecosystem integrity.

3. India's Diverse Avian Realms

3.1 From Mountain Peaks to Coastal Shores: A Mosaic of Habitats

The Himalayas, with their stark landscapes ranging from lush valleys to snow-capped peaks, host a plethora of avian species uniquely adapted to high altitudes. The iridescent Himalayan Monal (Lophophorus impejanus) thrives in the region's dense forests, foraging for insects, seeds, and roots. The elusive Snow Partridge (Lerwa lerwa) and the bone-eating Lammergeier (Gypaetus barbatus) also inhabit these high-altitude ecosystems, which are increasingly threatened by climate change and human encroachment.

Further south, the Western Ghats, a UNESCO World Heritage site, offer a rich mosaic of habitats from tropical rainforests to montane grasslands. Endemic species like the Nilgiri Flycatcher (Eumyias albicaudatus) and the Malabar Whistling Thrush (Myophonus horsfieldii) flourish here. The Great Hornbill (Buceros bicornis), a keystone species, underscores the critical need for conservation in these threatened forests.

The Eastern Ghats, though less continuous, provide crucial habitats for birds like the critically endangered Jerdon's Courser (Rhinoptilus bitorquatus). Conservation efforts focus on habitat protection amidst threats from agriculture and mining. Central India's plains, dominated by deciduous forests and grasslands, support the Indian Peafowl (Pavo cristatus) and the critically endangered Great Indian Bustard (Ardeotis nigriceps). These regions highlight the importance of conserving overlooked grasslands through protected areas and community-based programs.

In the fertile Gangetic Plains, wetlands like Keoladeo National Park are vital for migratory birds such as the Bar-headed Goose (Anser indicus) and the Sarus Crane (Antigone antigone). Conservation strategies here emphasize wetland protection and sustainable water management. The Thar Desert's arid conditions support species like the Indian Courser (Cursorius coromandelicus) and the Desert Lark (Ammomanes deserti), adapted to harsh climates and scarce water resources. Initiatives here focus on habitat protection and research. The Deccan Plateau's diverse habitats host endemic species like the Yellow-throated Bulbul (Pycnonotus xantholaemus). Conservation involves managing water resources and promoting sustainable agriculture.

Northeastern India's biodiverse forests, part of the Indo-Burma hotspot, shelter species like the Rufous-necked Hornbill (Aceros nipalensis). Conservation here addresses logging and infrastructure threats through community involvement. India's coastal regions, including the Sundarbans, are crucial for mangrove-dependent birds like the Brown-winged Kingfisher (Pelargopsis amauroptera). Protecting these ecosystems supports both biodiversity and local communities. The Andaman and Nicobar Islands' unique ecosystems host endemic species such as the Andaman Woodpecker (Dryocopus hodgei). Conservation focuses on habitat protection and invasive species control.

India's diverse avian habitats, from mountains to coasts, underscore the need for holistic conservation strategies addressing habitat degradation, climate change, and community engagement. Effective management of protected areas and community-based initiatives are essential for sustaining India's rich bird diversity.

3.2 A Symphony of Roles: Birds and their Ecosystem Services

Birds are pivotal pollinators in Indian ecosystems, from the Himalayan foothills to the Western Ghats. Species like sunbirds, hummingbirds, and certain parrots and pigeons facilitate plant reproduction through their foraging behaviors, ensuring plant diversity. Without these avian pollinators, many plants would struggle to reproduce, causing cascading effects on entire ecosystems. Additionally, birds are vital seed dispersers, particularly in forests. Species like hornbills, barbets, and mynas consume fruits and disperse seeds through their droppings, aiding in biodiversity and forest regeneration. This process supports the colonization of new areas by plants, playing a crucial role in ecosystem succession.

Birds also provide natural pest control. Insectivorous species such as sparrows, warblers, and flycatchers prey on pests that damage crops and forests, reducing the need for chemical pesticides and maintaining ecological balance. This service benefits agriculture and forest health alike. Moreover, birds contribute to nutrient cycling and soil health. Scavengers and omnivores accelerate decomposition by feeding on carrion and organic matter, returning nutrients to the soil. Bird droppings, rich in nitrogen and phosphorus, further enrich the soil and promote plant growth, especially in nutrient-poor ecosystems like grasslands and wetlands.

In aquatic environments, birds such as ducks, herons, and egrets play critical roles in nutrient cycling and water quality maintenance. Their feeding activities control populations of fish and invertebrates and disturb sediments, promoting nutrient recycling. The presence of waterbirds can also indicate the health of aquatic ecosystems, with declines serving as early warnings of habitat degradation. Beyond their ecological roles, birds hold cultural and economic significance in India. They inspire art, literature, and folklore, enriching the country's cultural heritage. Birdwatching tourism is a growing industry, attracting enthusiasts worldwide and providing livelihoods for local communities. The diversity of bird species in various habitats supports eco-tourism, contributing to local economies and fostering a deeper appreciation for the natural world.

4. India's Feathered Icons

4.1 The National Pride: The Majestic Indian Peafowl

The Indian Peafowl, known as the peacock, holds a revered status as India's "National Bird," emblematic of the nation's rich cultural heritage and biodiversity. Its resplendent appearance features iridescent blue-green plumage and elaborate tail feathers adorned with eye-spots, captivating both locals and visitors alike. Beyond its aesthetic allure, the Indian Peafowl plays crucial ecological roles within its native habitats. Found predominantly in forests, grasslands, and agricultural landscapes across India, these birds contribute significantly to seed dispersal and nutrient cycling through their diverse diet, which includes seeds, fruits, insects, and small invertebrates. By foraging on various plant materials, they help maintain the balance of local ecosystems.

Despite its cultural significance and ecological contributions, the Indian Peafowl faces formidable challenges across its range, imperiling its long-term survival. Habitat loss due to urbanization, agricultural expansion, and deforestation threatens peafowl populations by reducing available nesting and foraging sites, exacerbating competition for resources, and increasing vulnerability to predators and human disturbances. Additionally, illegal trade and poaching persistently threaten Indian Peafowl populations, driven by the demand for their feathers, meat, and live specimens. These activities undermine conservation efforts and perpetuate wildlife exploitation despite legal protections.

Human-wildlife conflicts further compound these challenges, particularly where peafowl interact with agricultural lands. During the breeding season, aggressive male behavior can lead to crop damage, escalating tensions between farmers and peafowls and sometimes resulting in retaliatory killings. Climate change poses an additional threat, altering weather patterns and habitat suitability across the peafowl's range. Shifts in temperature and precipitation can disrupt food availability and nesting success, while extreme weather events such as cyclones and droughts directly impact population dynamics.

Efforts to conserve the Indian Peafowl require comprehensive strategies addressing habitat preservation, mitigation of human-wildlife conflicts, enforcement of anti-poaching laws, and adaptation to climate change impacts. Protecting these iconic birds not only safeguards their cultural and ecological significance but also promotes the conservation of India's natural heritage for future generations.

4.2 Beyond the Peacock: Celebrating Other Endemic Species

India's avian diversity extends far beyond the majestic Indian Peafowl, encompassing a wealth of endemic bird species deserving of admiration and conservation efforts. From the towering Himalayan peaks to the lush Western Ghats, these birds have evolved unique adaptations to their habitats, enriching India's avifauna. Among these treasures is the Indian Pitta (Pitta brachyura), renowned for its vibrant plumage and melodious calls. Inhabiting central and southern India's forests and scrublands, this ground-dwelling bird forages amidst leaf litter for insects and small invertebrates. However, habitat loss threatens its survival as deforestation diminishes suitable breeding and foraging grounds.

Equally captivating is the Nilgiri Laughingthrush (Montecincla cachinnans), endemic to the shola-grassland habitats of the Western Ghats. With striking black-and-orange plumage and raucous calls, this bird epitomizes the unique biodiversity of the Nilgiri Hills. Yet, habitat fragmentation and climate change jeopardize its future, underscoring the need for habitat conservation efforts. In northeastern India, the Bugun Liocichla (*Liocichla bugunorum*) serves as a conservation success story. Discovered in 2006 in Arunachal Pradesh's Eaglenest Wildlife Sanctuary, this bird's vivid blue, yellow, and black plumage spurred local and international conservation initiatives. Protecting its montane forest habitat from logging and anthropogenic activities remains critical to its survival.

In the arid landscapes of western India, the Great Indian Bustard (*Ardeotis nigriceps*) faces severe threats. Once abundant across grasslands and semi-arid plains, habitat loss, fragmentation, and hunting have decimated its population. Urgent conservation measures, including habitat restoration and community involvement, are essential to prevent its extinction. The Narcondam Hornbill (*Aceros narcondami*), endemic to Narcondam Island in the Andaman and Nicobar Islands, exemplifies the unique biodiversity of these remote archipelagos. Vital for seed dispersal and forest regeneration, this species confronts habitat destruction from logging, agriculture, and invasive species. Protecting its forest habitat and controlling invasive species are imperative to ensure its survival.

These endemic birds not only highlight India's natural heritage but also underscore the importance of concerted conservation efforts to safeguard their future amidst mounting environmental challenges.

5. Avian Adaptations: Thriving in Diverse Environments

5.1 Specialized for Survival: Unique Adaptations of Indian Birds

In the diverse landscapes of India, birds exhibit remarkable adaptations tailored to their environments. In the arid expanses of western India, the Indian Eagle-Owl (*Bubo bengalensis*) employs its large size and insulated plumage to regulate body heat and minimize water loss amidst fluctuating temperatures. Nocturnal by nature, it adeptly hunts in darkness with its keen senses and silent flight, evading the harsh daytime conditions. At higher elevations in the Himalayas, the Himalayan Monal (*Lophophorus impejanus*) thrives with specialized adaptations to low-oxygen environments. Enhanced respiratory systems and increased red blood cell production enable efficient oxygen extraction from thin mountain air. Its cryptic plumage camouflages it against rocky terrain, while territorial behaviors secure vital resources in the alpine ecosystem.

In the dense rainforests of the Western Ghats, the Malabar Trogon (*Harpactes fasciatus*) maneuvers effortlessly through the canopy with its slender build and agile movements. Vibrant plumage provides effective camouflage, aiding in prey capture among dappled sunlight and shadows. Strong claws and flexible joints ensure secure perching and precise prey snatching in the arboreal habitat. In eastern India's wetlands, the Asian Openbill (*Anastomus oscitans*) thrives with its distinctive bill adapted for probing mud and catching aquatic prey like mollusks and fish. Broad wings and long legs facilitate graceful gliding over water and wading through marshy landscapes, showcasing prowess in wetland ecosystems.

Along southern India's coasts, the Brahminy Kite (*Haliastur indus*) utilizes hooked beaks and sharp talons to hunt fish and scavenges carrion. Excellent eyesight aids in spotting prey from afar, while streamlined bodies and broad wings conserve energy during coastal flights. In urban environments nationwide, the House Sparrow (*Passer domesticus*) has adapted to coexist with humans. Opportunistic feeding and nesting behaviors in parks, gardens, and residential areas sustain its population despite challenges like habitat loss and pollution.

These avian adaptations illustrate their remarkable resilience and ability to thrive across India's diverse landscapes, reflecting their evolutionary responses to environmental challenges.

5.2 Birds on the Move: Understanding Migration Patterns in India

Bird migration is a captivating phenomenon that profoundly shapes India's avian landscape, with millions of birds annually traversing the country in search of food, breeding grounds, and favorable climates. Studying these migration patterns is crucial for conservation and ecosystem management, offering insights into habitat connectivity, species distribution, and the impacts of environmental changes on bird populations. India serves as a vital stopover and wintering ground for a diverse array of migratory birds, intersected by major flyways such as the Central Asian, East Asian-Australasian, and East Atlantic routes. These pathways link wetlands, coastal areas, forests, and grasslands, providing essential refueling and resting sites for migratory birds.

An iconic example is the Siberian Crane (Grus leucogeranus), undertaking a perilous journey of over 6,000 kilometers from Siberia to India's wetlands, notably Bharatpur and Keoladeo National Park, to escape harsh winters. However, their population has dwindled due to habitat loss, hunting, and disturbances along migration routes. Similarly, the Amur Falcon (Falco amurensis) captures attention with its spectacular migration across India to southern Africa, facing threats like habitat destruction and electrocution on power lines.

Migratory shorebirds such as the Bar-tailed Godwit (Limosa lapponica) and Eurasian Curlew (Numenius arquata) rely on India's coastal wetlands during their non-stop flights across oceans, threatened by habitat degradation and human activities. India hosts various short-distance migrants like the Rosy Starling (Pastor roseus) and altitudinal migrants such as the Rufous-bellied Niltava (Niltava sundara), adapting within the country based on seasonal changes.

Comprehensive research involving bird banding, satellite tracking, and citizen science is pivotal, with organizations like the Bombay Natural History Society (BNHS) and Indian Bird Conservation Network (IBCN) monitoring populations and advocating for migratory habitat conservation. International collaborations like the Convention on Migratory Species (CMS) and Ramsar Convention on Wetlands facilitate transboundary efforts to safeguard migratory birds and their habitats. Understanding India's bird migration intricacies requires concerted conservation actions and public awareness initiatives.

DATA SHEET - II
TRENDS AND CHALLENGES IN INDIA'S BIRD POPULATIONS

Study Insight	Key Findings	Citation
State of India's Birds: 60% population decline amid habitat and food loss, changing ecosystems	☐ A majority of bird species in India are on the decline, indicating alarming biodiversity loss and anthropogenic pressures ☐ 60% of 348 bird species assessed showed long-term declines, and 40% are currently declining	[2]
Birds living in open habitat seeing declining trend, large number of common species in trouble: report	☐ 60% of India's 338 bird species have declined in the long-term ☐ 40% of species have declined in the past 7 years ☐ Generalist species increased, but habitat specialists, carnivores, insectivores, and granivores are declining rapidly	[3]

State of India's Birds 2023: Conservation Of 178 Species Should Be Highly Prioritised, Says New Study	□ 60% of 348 species assessed show long-term declines □ 40% of species are currently declining □ Conservation of 178 bird species should be highly prioritised	[4]
India's Birds in Crisis: 50% at Risk Due to Climate Change, Deforestation	□ India's avian diversity is under threat, with climate change and deforestation leading to the potential loss of 50% of bird species	[5]
India's declining birdlife	□ The report assesses the status of Indian birds not usually covered by conservation efforts or data □ It has used citizen science as its database, collaborating with national research and conservation organisations	[6]
Seabird conservation status, threats and priority actions: a global assessment	- Seabirds are more threatened than other comparable groups of birds, and their conservation status has deteriorated faster over recent decades □ The principal threats to seabirds at sea are posed by commercial fisheries, pollution, and at land, by alien invasive predators, habitat degradation, and human disturbance	[7]
Role of India's wildlife in the emergence and re-emergence of zoonotic pathogens, risk factors and public health implications	- Evolving land use practices have led to an increase in interactions at the human-wildlife interface, with diverse migratory bird populations playing a role - In the emergence and re-emergence of zoonotic pathogens	[8]
Conservation challenges of wet-tropical nature	- Protected areas in the Northeast region of India face significant anthropogenic pressure	[9]

reserves in north-east India	from habitat loss, fragmentation, and hunting - The complex socio-economic and cultural context in the region, including deep-rooted hunting practices, pose additional challenges	
Retreating Wild Mammals of Pune Urban Area	- Habitat loss due to urbanization has affected about one-third of the mammal species in the Pune urban area - Pollution, hunting, poaching, and superstitions leading to the persecution of certain species have also contributed to wildlife declines	[10]
Birds Face Extinction Risk Due To Human Activities	- Human activities have caused some 500 bird species worldwide to go extinct over the past five millennia, and 21st-century extinction rates are likely to accelerate	[11]
Urbanization and Its Impact on Avian Diversity in Indian Cities	☐ Urbanization leads to habitat loss, fragmentation, and pollution, which severely impact avian diversity in Indian cities ☐ Certain species adapt while others face significant decline	[12]
Agricultural Expansion and Pesticide Use in India: Threats to Bird Populations	☐ Agricultural expansion and pesticide use are major threats to bird populations in India ☐ Decline in insectivorous bird species observed due to pesticide use	[13]
Impact of Climate Change on Migratory Birds in India	☐ Climate change is altering migration patterns, breeding seasons, and habitats of migratory birds in India ☐ Increased mortality rates and population declines observed in migratory species	[14]

Conservation Strategies for the Indian Vulture Population	☐ Indian vulture populations have plummeted due to the use of the drug diclofenac ☐ Conservation efforts include banning the drug and establishing vulture safe zones	[15]
Habitat Fragmentation and its Effects on Bird Species in Western Ghats	☐ Habitat fragmentation in the Western Ghats has led to decreased bird diversity ☐ Endemic species are particularly vulnerable to fragmentation	[16]
Effects of Monoculture Plantations on Bird Populations in Northeast India	☐ Monoculture plantations negatively impact bird populations by reducing habitat complexity and food availability ☐ Native species show significant decline in plantation areas	[17]
Avian Response to Forest Management Practices in Central India	☐ Different forest management practices, such as selective logging and clear-cutting, have varied impacts on bird species ☐ Sustainable practices can mitigate negative effects on bird populations	[18]
Impact of Invasive Plant Species on Bird Diversity in the Andaman Islands	☐ Invasive plant species outcompete native vegetation, leading to habitat loss for native bird species ☐ Significant decline in endemic bird populations observed	[19]
Breeding Success of Wetland Birds in the Face of Water Pollution	☐ Water pollution from agricultural runoff and industrial discharge negatively affects the breeding success of wetland birds ☐ Reduced chick survival rates and deformities observed in polluted areas	[20]
The Role of Sacred Groves in Conserving Avian Biodiversity in India	☐ Sacred groves serve as important refuges for bird species,	[21]

	preserving biodiversity in fragmented landscapes ☐ Traditional conservation practices contribute to higher bird diversity in these areas	
Impact of Noise Pollution on Urban Birds in India	☐ Noise pollution disrupts communication, breeding, and feeding behaviors of urban birds ☐ Species that rely heavily on vocal communication are most affected	[22]
Seasonal Migration Patterns of the Indian Roller and Challenges Faced	☐ Indian Roller migration patterns are affected by habitat loss and climate change ☐ Increased mortality rates during migration due to habitat fragmentation and extreme weather events	[23]
Avian Influenza and its Impact on Bird Populations in India	☐ Avian influenza outbreaks lead to significant mortality in both wild and domesticated bird populations Surveillance and rapid response strategies are critical to managing outbreaks	[24]

CHAPTER 2

The Looming Crisis: Challenges Faced by India's Birds

1. Habitat Loss and Degradation: A Shrinking Sanctuary

1.1 Development's Toll: Urbanization, Agriculture, and Deforestation

The rapid urbanization and agricultural expansion in India pose profound challenges to its avian biodiversity, exacerbated by deforestation. Urbanization transforms natural habitats into sprawling cities, replacing forests, wetlands, and grasslands with concrete landscapes. This urban sprawl diminishes essential bird habitats, restricting nesting, foraging, and roosting opportunities amid increasing noise and light pollution, disrupting bird behaviors and migration patterns. As cities encroach upon rural areas, wetlands crucial for many bird species are drained for urban development, depriving birds of vital resources like food and nesting sites. Habitat fragmentation isolates green spaces into small, unsustainable patches, heightening predation risks and limiting mate availability, further imperiling bird populations.

Agricultural intensification exacerbates habitat loss, replacing diverse ecosystems with monoculture farms devoid of the plant and insect diversity essential for avian diets. Chemical pesticides and fertilizers further deplete insect populations critical to many birds, while deforestation for agriculture eradicates vital forest habitats, disrupting ecosystems and diminishing bird populations reliant on these environments. Deforestation, driven by agricultural expansion and resource extraction, eliminates crucial bird habitats, fragmenting forests and disrupting ecological balances essential for bird survival. The loss of forest cover alters local climates and water cycles, impacting habitat quality through soil erosion and reduced water availability, particularly affecting ground-foraging bird species.

Moreover, urbanization, agriculture, and deforestation facilitate the spread of invasive species, competing with native flora and fauna for resources and altering habitat compositions detrimental to indigenous bird populations. These factors collectively contribute to habitat degradation and population declines among India's diverse avian species, highlighting urgent conservation needs to mitigate these impacts.

1.2 Fragmentation's Impact: Isolating Populations and Disrupting Connectivity

Fragmentation of habitats poses a profound threat to India's avian diversity, disrupting ecological connectivity and imperiling bird populations. As development expands, large, contiguous habitats are increasingly divided into smaller, isolated patches by roads, railways, and other infrastructure. These barriers hinder birds' movements, separating populations into smaller groups that face heightened risks such as genetic depletion and susceptibility to environmental pressures. Isolated populations are particularly vulnerable to local extinction due to their increased exposure to disease outbreaks, extreme weather events, and human disturbances. Inbreeding can further diminish genetic diversity, exacerbating their precarious status. Reduced ability to disperse and colonize new habitats further threatens survival, limiting access to essential resources like food and nesting sites and diminishing reproductive success.

Migration routes are severely impacted by habitat fragmentation, disrupting vital stopover sites crucial for resting and refueling during long journeys. Loss of these sites increases mortality rates among migratory birds, as they struggle to find adequate food and shelter along fragmented paths. The stress of navigating altered landscapes can also reduce migratory birds' survival rates and overall health.

The ecological repercussions extend beyond bird populations, affecting pollination, seed dispersal, and pest control crucial for ecosystem health. Disrupted movements of birds can lead to cascading effects on plant and insect communities, altering biodiversity dynamics. Edge effects at habitat boundaries further compound issues, altering resource availability and increasing susceptibility to invasive species and predation. While some bird species show resilience in fragmented landscapes, others, particularly forest-dwelling species, face heightened vulnerability. Effective conservation strategies must prioritize maintaining and restoring habitat connectivity. Establishing wildlife corridors-vegetated strips along roads, rivers, and protected lands-can facilitate movement and bolster genetic diversity. Restoring degraded habitats through reforestation, afforestation, and wetland restoration is critical to supporting bird populations and mitigating fragmentation's impact.

Community involvement is pivotal, fostering stewardship and support for conservation efforts. Educating and engaging local communities in habitat restoration and monitoring initiatives can enhance conservation effectiveness. Policy reforms are essential, emphasizing habitat protection and integrating environmental impact assessments into development planning to safeguard bird habitats and promote connectivity. By prioritizing habitat connectivity and engaging communities and policymakers, conservation efforts can mitigate the adverse effects of habitat fragmentation, ensuring the long-term survival of India's diverse bird populations.

2. The Shadow of Pollution: A Toxic Threat to Avian Health

2.1 Industrial Effluents and Agricultural Runoff: Poisoning Water Sources

Industrial effluents and agricultural runoff pose significant threats to avian health in India by contaminating crucial water sources essential for drinking, feeding, and breeding. The rapid industrialization and intensified agricultural practices have resulted in the discharge of various pollutants into rivers, lakes, and wetlands, vital habitats for numerous bird species. These pollutants encompass heavy metals, pesticides, fertilizers, and other chemicals detrimental to both bird populations and their ecosystems. Industrial effluents, often released untreated or inadequately treated into water bodies, are primary sources of water pollution. They frequently contain toxic heavy metals like mercury, lead, and cadmium, even in trace amounts, which adversely affect birds upon ingestion through contaminated water or prey. Exposure to heavy metals can impair neurological functions, hindering coordination, foraging, and migration. Chronic exposure further diminishes reproductive success by causing issues such as eggshell thinning and developmental abnormalities in chicks.

In addition to heavy metals, industrial effluents introduce organic pollutants like polycyclic aromatic hydrocarbons (PAHs) and polychlorinated biphenyls (PCBs) into the environment. These persistent compounds bioaccumulate in the food chain, reaching high concentrations in top avian predators. PAHs and PCBs disrupt endocrine systems, impacting hormone regulation and leading to reproductive and developmental complications in birds, including reduced fertility and compromised immune function.

Agricultural runoff exacerbates water pollution by leaching chemical pesticides and fertilizers into nearby water bodies. Pesticides designed to control pests also harm non-target species like birds, causing acute poisoning symptoms such as tremors and convulsions, and can lead to chronic health issues like weakened immune systems and reproductive failure. Fertilizers rich in nitrogen and phosphorus contribute to eutrophication, stimulating excessive algae growth. Decomposing algae then deplete oxygen levels in water, threatening fish-eating and insectivorous bird species dependent on these habitats.

The cumulative impact of multiple pollutants, compounded by habitat loss and climate change, intensifies threats to bird populations. Wetlands, crucial for diverse bird species including waterfowl and migratory birds, are particularly vulnerable. Pollution degrades wetland quality, diminishing biodiversity and impairing ecosystem functions vital for bird survival. Birds serve as sensitive indicators of environmental health, reflecting the extent and effects of water pollution. Monitoring bird populations provides insights into pollution impacts, guiding conservation efforts and policies aimed at safeguarding avian health and ecosystem integrity.

2.2 Beyond Water: Air Pollution and Electromagnetic Radiation Concerns

Air pollution and electromagnetic radiation pose significant threats to avian health in India, necessitating urgent attention. While water pollution's impacts are well-documented, the effects of airborne pollutants and electromagnetic fields on birds remain critical areas of concern. These environmental stressors disrupt birds' physiology, behavior, and ecological roles, jeopardizing populations and biodiversity. Urban areas in India face alarming levels of air pollution, driven by industrial activities, vehicular emissions, and construction dust. Key pollutants include particulate matter (PM), sulfur dioxide (SO_2), nitrogen oxides (NO_x), carbon monoxide (CO), and ozone (O_3). Birds, with their high respiratory rates and extensive respiratory surfaces, are particularly vulnerable. PM2.5 and PM10 can penetrate deep into their respiratory systems, causing inflammation and impairing oxygen exchange, which can be fatal, especially for smaller species.

Sulfur dioxide and nitrogen oxides, contributing to acid rain formation, affect aquatic habitats crucial for many bird species. Acidification alters water and soil pH, impacting nutrient availability and ecosystem health. These pollutants can damage feathers and reduce insulation, exposing birds to harsh weather conditions. Chronic exposure weakens immune systems, increasing susceptibility to diseases. Ground-level ozone, formed through sunlight reacting with VOCs and nitrogen oxides, further threatens avian respiratory health and foraging abilities. Carbon monoxide, from incomplete fossil fuel combustion, disrupts oxygen transport in birds' blood, leading to hypoxia and impaired flight abilities. Pollutants also accumulate in food chains, causing biomagnification and further health risks for birds.

Electromagnetic radiation, primarily from telecom infrastructure, poses additional risks. Birds relying on Earth's magnetic field for navigation can become disoriented by artificial EMFs, leading to navigation errors and increased collision risks with structures. High EMF exposure alters hormone levels, reduces reproductive success, and weakens immune systems, impacting overall bird fitness and behavior. In response, mitigating these impacts requires comprehensive strategies. These include stricter industrial emission controls, promoting cleaner energy sources, and enhancing urban green spaces to absorb pollutants. Addressing electromagnetic radiation risks involves thoughtful placement of infrastructure and reducing unnecessary exposure through technological innovations.

Balancing development with environmental protection is crucial to safeguarding avian populations and biodiversity in India's rapidly urbanizing landscape. Integrating scientific research, policy interventions, and public awareness efforts can mitigate these threats and ensure sustainable coexistence between birds and human activities.

3. Climate Change: A Shifting Landscape

3.1 Rising Temperatures and Altered Rainfall Patterns: Disrupting Habitats

Rising temperatures pose a significant threat to bird habitats across India, impacting species from the Himalayan mountains to the arid plains of Rajasthan and Gujarat. Birds, reliant on specific temperature ranges for survival and reproduction, face physiological stress as temperatures exceed their tolerance limits. For instance, elevated temperatures can disrupt incubation processes, leading to reduced hatching success among various species. Moreover, shifting phenology of food sources due to climate change further challenges bird populations. Many birds time their breeding to coincide with peak food availability, but altered temperatures can cause mismatches in these cycles, resulting in higher chick mortality and reduced parental fitness. In high-altitude Himalayan regions, rising temperatures contribute to glacier retreat and diminished snow cover, shrinking habitats for cold-adapted species like the snow partridge and Himalayan monal, potentially leading to local extinctions.

In arid regions like Rajasthan and Gujarat, increased temperatures exacerbate water scarcity, critical for hydration and nesting. Birds such as the Indian courser and great Indian bustard, already under threat from habitat loss, must travel longer distances for water, impacting their reproductive success. Altered rainfall patterns, another consequence of climate change, significantly affect bird habitats across diverse landscapes. Wetland habitats crucial for migratory birds like the Siberian crane are vulnerable to drying due to erratic rainfall. In the Western Ghats, unpredictable rainfall alters forest structure, affecting endemic species such as the Malabar grey hornbill and Nilgiri flycatcher.

The monsoon, vital for replenishing India's water resources, is becoming increasingly erratic. Delayed monsoon arrivals disrupt breeding cycles for waterfowl dependent on wetland habitats. Excessive rainfall can flood nests and reduce suitable nesting sites for ground-nesting species. In agricultural landscapes, changes in rainfall patterns influence crop growth, impacting birds that forage in fields for food. Birds like the Indian roller and black-headed ibis face food shortages when crops fail due to inadequate or excessive rainfall.

Coastal mangrove ecosystems, home to species like the mangrove whistler and brown-winged kingfisher, are also affected by altered rainfall. Changes in freshwater availability due to shifting rainfall patterns can disrupt the delicate balance of saltwater and freshwater essential for mangrove health and bird survival.

3.2 The Challenge of Adaptation: Impeding Migration Routes and Breeding Cycles

Climate change profoundly impacts bird populations, especially through disruptions in migration routes. Migration, finely tuned by evolutionary adaptations to seasonal climate variations, relies on cues like temperature changes and daylight length. As global temperatures rise and weather patterns become erratic, these cues increasingly fall out of sync with historical norms, affecting migration timing and leading to ecological consequences. Migratory birds depend on specific stopover sites for crucial resources such as food and shelter, typically found in wetlands or coastal areas. Climate change alters these habitats, potentially drying wetlands or altering rainfall patterns, reducing food and water availability. This forces birds like the bar-headed goose and black-tailed godwit to travel farther without adequate rest, impacting their energy and fitness.

Moreover, climate change affects food availability along migration routes. Birds time their travels to coincide with peak food availability, like insects or fruits. However, mismatches caused by early insect emergence or shifts in food availability can lead to inadequate nutrition, affecting migration success and breeding. The Eurasian spoonbill, reliant on specific wetlands for feeding during migration, faces survival risks from prey availability disruptions. Breeding cycles are also disrupted by climate change, crucial for species like the Indian pitta and Malabar grey hornbill, whose food sources and nesting conditions are affected. Rising temperatures can make traditional nesting sites unsuitable, impacting birds such as the ground-nesting Indian courser or tree-cavity nesting brown-headed barbet. Extreme weather events exacerbated by climate change, like storms or heatwaves, pose additional threats, destroying nests and causing direct mortality among eggs and chicks. The endangered great Indian bustard, nesting on open grasslands, and seabirds like the black-bellied tern nesting on coastal areas, are particularly vulnerable to such events, affecting their populations severely.

4. The Peril of Exploitation: Poaching, Illegal Trade, and Collisions

4.1 Poaching and Illegal Trade: The Loss of Valuable Birds and Biodiversity

Poaching, the illegal hunting, capturing, and killing of birds, remains a persistent threat driven by various motives such as the demand for bird parts in traditional medicine, the pet trade, and the use of feathers for adornments and rituals. Among the most targeted species is the Indian peafowl, prized for its vibrant feathers despite legal protections under India's Wildlife Protection Act. This ongoing poaching not only jeopardizes the peafowl's population but also disrupts ecosystems where they play crucial roles in seed dispersal and pest control.

Similarly, the demand for exotic pets fuels the illegal capture of species like parrots, mynas, and hornbills. The Indian ring-necked parakeet, favored in the pet trade, suffers from frequent illegal capture, impacting both wild populations and social structures critical for breeding success. Hornbills, such as the great hornbill and the Malabar pied hornbill, face threats due to poaching for their casques and feathers, diminishing their vital role in forest ecosystems as seed dispersers. The illicit bird trade thrives on international demand, often subjecting birds to harsh transport conditions and high mortality rates. For instance, the Asian openbill stork suffers greatly during smuggling attempts, affecting its population in wetland habitats essential for biodiversity.

Raptors like eagles, hawks, and owls also fall victim to poaching, driven by superstitions and traditional beliefs. The loss of these top predators can disrupt ecological balance, affecting pest control and agricultural health by allowing unchecked increases in prey populations. Beyond poaching, collisions with urban infrastructure pose another grave threat to bird populations. Birds frequently collide with glass windows and reflective surfaces in high-rise buildings, while power lines and wind turbines also contribute to significant mortality, especially among larger species and migratory birds.

Communication towers with steady burning lights attract and disorient migratory birds, further increasing collision risks, especially in foggy conditions. Additionally, the expansion of road networks and railways amplifies collisions with vehicles, threatening species that forage near roadsides. Balancing conservation efforts with developmental needs is crucial to mitigate these threats, ensuring the preservation of India's diverse bird species and their invaluable ecological contributions.

5. Human-Wildlife Conflict: Sharing Space with Challenges

5.1 Crop Raiding and Property Damage: Understanding Bird Behavior

Birds like parakeets, crows, and mynas frequently engage in crop raiding throughout India, targeting crops such as maize, rice, and fruits like mangoes and grapes. Their foraging behavior is influenced by seasonal food availability, breeding cycles, and habitat fragmentation. During crop ripening seasons, these birds often concentrate in agricultural areas, resulting in significant losses for farmers. Predicting these patterns aids in implementing preemptive measures. The economic impact of crop raiding by birds is considerable, causing direct losses through reduced yield and quality, and indirect costs from deterrent measures like nets and scare devices. These losses can jeopardize food security and exacerbate poverty in farming communities. Therefore, mitigating crop raiding is both an ecological necessity and an economic imperative. Studies of bird behavior reveal species-specific foraging habits and adaptability. Parakeets, for example, are adept at accessing fruits at various ripeness stages, while crows target grains during planting or harvesting periods. This understanding allows for targeted interventions such as adjusting planting schedules or cultivating bird-resistant crop varieties. Bird-related property damage extends beyond fields to urban areas, where species like pigeons and mynas nest in residential and commercial buildings, causing noise, fouling, and structural damage. Addressing these conflicts requires understanding urban bird behavior and implementing effective deterrent strategies.

Efforts to manage crop raiding and property damage must balance human interests with the ecological roles of birds in pollination, seed dispersal, and pest control. Sustainable solutions emphasize coexistence over eradication, integrating traditional practices like scarecrows with modern technologies such as lasers and drones for enhanced efficacy and reduced operational costs.

DATA SHEET - III
IMPACT OF HABITAT LOSS ON AVIAN SPECIES IN INDIA

Study Title	Key Findings	Citation
Significant bird records and local extinctions in Purna and Ratanmahal Wildlife Sanctuaries, Gujarat, India	Loss, fragmentation, and degradation of habitat have led to local extinctions and significant impacts on bird species.	[25]
Loss of biodiversity and conservation strategies: an outlook of Indian scenario	Extensive habitat degradation in coastal regions, affecting a range of bird species and other fauna.	[26]
Biodiversity loss and its Ecological impact in India	Habitat loss and forest degradation significantly affect birds requiring large territories and migratory habits.	[27]
Rapid degradation of wetlands and its impact on avifauna: A case study from Ambuja Wetland, West Bengal, India	Rapid urban transformation significantly affects wetland birds.	[28]

Decline of coastal birds along the south-east coast of India	Coastal habitat loss and degradation have severely impacted wintering bird species, particularly Arctic breeding sandpipers.	[29]
Decline in forest bird species and guilds due to land use change in the Western Himalaya	Degraded forests support fewer bird species; changes in land use have significantly affected bird populations.	[30]
Global trends of habitat destruction and consequences for parrot conservation	Forest loss and degradation in India and other regions affect habitat availability for parrots and other birds.	[31]
Birds of the Kangchenjunga Landscape, the Eastern Himalaya: status, threats and implications for conservation	Habitat destruction, fragmentation, and degradation have significant impacts on bird diversity in the Eastern Himalaya.	[32]
Habitat change and biodiversity loss in South and Southeast Asian countries	India experiences significant biodiversity loss due to habitat destruction and degradation.	[33]
Biodiversity significance of small habitat patches: More than half of Indian bird species are in academic campuses	Small habitat patches in urban areas play a crucial role in conserving bird diversity amidst habitat loss.	[34]
Unreported yet massive deforestation driving loss of endemic biodiversity in Indian Himalaya	Massive deforestation in the Indian Himalaya leads to loss of bird species and habitat degradation.	[35]
Effects of habitat degradation on mixed-species bird flocks in Indian forests	Habitat degradation affects the composition and dynamics of mixed-species bird flocks in Indian forests through changes in the bird community and resource availability.	[35]
Bird Species diversity from the Southern West part of West Bengal, India	A study that identified 343 bird species in the Southwest part of West Bengal, India, highlighting the high species	[36]

	diversity and the need for conservation efforts in the region.	
Transitioning Wintering Shorebirds to Agroecosystem: A Thorough Evaluation of Habitat Selection and Conservation Concern	This study found that 53 shorebird species utilize diverse agroecosystems in different parts of India, emphasizing the importance of sustainable agricultural practices for the conservation of these migratory birds.	[37]
Composition and status of avian diversity in the Mandothi wetland habitat of Jhajjar, Haryana, India	The study documented 133 bird species in the Mandothi Wetlands, Haryana, India, including one endangered and one vulnerable species, highlighting the importance of conserving these wetland habitats.	[37]
Raptors and linear infrastructure in Chhattisgarh, India: species composition and conservation concern	This study identified 14 raptor species in northern Chhattisgarh, India, including two threatened species, and emphasized the need for appropriate measures to mitigate the negative effects of linear infrastructure development on bird populations.	[38]
Birds of the Kangchenjunga Landscape, the Eastern Himalaya: status, threats and implications for conservation	The study reviewed the bird species of the Kangchenjunga Landscape in the Eastern Himalaya, which is a transboundary region shared by Bhutan, India, and Nepal. It identified numerous threats to the birds, including habitat loss and fragmentation, and provided recommendations for conservation strategies.	[32]
Diversity, composition and conservation status of avian fauna in the forest and the wetland sites of Hastinapur wildlife sanctuary, India	This study found that the wetland habitat in the Hastinapur Wildlife Sanctuary had higher bird species richness and abundance compared to the forest habitat, highlighting the importance of wetland conservation for avian diversity.	[39]
Composition and Conservation Status of Avifauna in Urban Non-protected Important	The study examined the avifauna of the Kumbharwada wetland, an Important Bird Area in Bhavnagar, Gujarat, India, and found that it supports a diverse bird	[39]

Bird Area (IBA) Site of Western India	community, including several globally threatened species.	
Birds living in open habitat seeing declining trend, large number of common species in trouble: report	A report that highlights the declining trend of bird populations in India, with 60% of the 338 bird species studied showing long-term declines, and 40% declining in the past 7 years.	[40]
Birds Species plummeting in India, says new report: What are the major threats to them?	This report discusses the major threats to bird species in India, including habitat loss, urbanization, infrastructure development, and climate change, leading to the decline of bird populations.	[41]
48% of bird species declining globally; 50% declining strongly in India	This report found that populations of almost half of all bird species are declining globally due to human-influenced factors, such as habitat loss or degradation, and that 50% of bird species in India are declining strongly.	[42]
Logging and Habitat Degradation: Conserving Wildlife	This article provides a case study demonstrating the impact of logging on bird species richness and abundance in a tropical rainforest, highlighting the critical issue of habitat degradation for wildlife conservation.	[43]

CHAPTER 3

Habitat Loss and Degradation : A Deeper Dive

1. A Symphony of Ecosystems: Understanding Bird Habitats in India

1.1 From Lush Forests to Coastal Wetlands: Diverse Homes for Avian Life

India's landscapes, from dense forests to coastal wetlands, offer a remarkable variety of habitats that support an extensive array of avian life. Understanding these habitats is essential for addressing the conservation challenges birds face and tailoring effective strategies for each ecosystem. Lush Forests: Spanning tropical rainforests in the Western Ghats to central India's deciduous forests, these habitats host a staggering diversity of bird species. The Indian paradise flycatcher and Malabar trogon thrive here, relying on dense foliage for nesting and feeding. However, deforestation, logging, and fragmentation threaten these areas, disrupting bird populations and ecological processes. Conservation efforts focus on establishing protected areas, promoting sustainable forestry, and restoring degraded lands.

Arid and Semi-Arid Scrublands: The Thar Desert and the scrublands of Rajasthan and Gujarat present unique challenges. Species like the Indian bustard and the Great Indian desert wheatear have evolved to cope with limited water and extreme temperatures. These habitats face pressures from grazing, agriculture, and infrastructure development. Efforts emphasize habitat restoration, water management, and community engagement to support these specialized bird populations. Coastal Wetlands: India's coastlines, estuaries, mangroves, and salt marshes are among the most biodiverse avian habitats. Migratory birds, including flamingos and shorebirds, rely on these wetlands for stopovers and wintering grounds. Urbanization, pollution, aquaculture, and climate change pose significant threats. Conservation initiatives focus on designating Ramsar sites, implementing coastal management plans, and promoting sustainable aquaculture to protect these critical habitats.

Agricultural Landscapes: Rice paddies, wheat fields, and orchards provide vital resources for both resident and migratory birds like sparrows and Indian rollers. Intensive farming practices, pesticides, and monoculture farming pose significant challenges. Promoting agroecological practices, such as organic farming and integrated pest management, alongside creating bird-friendly habitats, can enhance the ecological value of these landscapes. Urban and Suburban Environments: Cities and towns offer habitats for adaptable species like pigeons and mynas. However, urbanization brings risks, including habitat fragmentation, pollution, and collisions with buildings. Conservation efforts in urban areas include urban greening, rooftop gardens, bird-friendly architecture, and public awareness campaigns. Integrated planning and community engagement are crucial for balancing urban development with bird conservation.

1.2 The Interdependence of Nature: Birds and their Ecosystem Roles

Birds are integral to India's diverse ecosystems, contributing significantly to ecological balance and functioning. Their roles in pollination, seed dispersal, pest control, nutrient cycling, habitat engineering, and as indicator species highlight their interdependence with nature and the intricate web of relationships sustaining biodiversity and human well-being. Pollination and Seed Dispersal: Birds such as sunbirds, flowerpeckers, and hummingbirds are vital pollinators, especially in tropical forests and gardens. Their visits to flowers for nectar transfer pollen, promoting genetic diversity and fruit production. Frugivorous birds like bulbuls and pigeons disperse seeds through their droppings, aiding in forest regeneration and maintaining plant diversity. Loss of these bird-mediated processes disrupts plant reproduction cycles, affecting entire ecosystems.

Pest Control: Birds provide natural pest control by preying on insects, rodents, and other invertebrates. Raptors like owls and eagles regulate rodent populations in agricultural landscapes, while wading birds such as herons and egrets maintain aquatic ecosystem health by feeding on fish and amphibians. This natural pest control reduces the need for chemical pesticides, minimizing environmental contamination and promoting sustainable agriculture. Nutrient Cycling: Birds enhance nutrient cycling by depositing organic matter through their droppings, enriching soils and promoting plant growth. Colonial nesting birds, like seabirds, create nutrient-rich guano deposits on islands and coastal cliffs, supporting vegetation. In forests, roosting birds contribute essential nutrients to the soil, vital for maintaining fertility and agricultural productivity.

Ecosystem Engineers: Certain birds, such as woodpeckers and burrowing species like Indian rollers, modify habitats through their behaviors, creating niches for other species and enhancing habitat complexity. These modifications contribute to biodiversity and ecosystem resilience. Indicator Species: Birds are sensitive indicators of environmental health, reflecting changes in habitat quality, pollution, and climate conditions. Shifts in bird populations can signal broader ecological disruptions, informing conservation actions to mitigate threats like habitat loss and climate change. Cultural and Ecotourism Value: Birds hold significant cultural and ecotourism value in India, attracting birdwatchers and nature enthusiasts. Protected areas conserve bird habitats, fostering birdwatching and ecotourism activities that generate economic benefits and promote conservation awareness. Supporting sustainable tourism practices ensures these benefits while respecting bird habitats.

Understanding and protecting these avian roles is crucial for maintaining India's ecological integrity and promoting biodiversity conservation.

2. The Price of Progress: Analyzing Habitat Loss and its Consequences

2.1 Deforestation's Devastation: Loss of Nesting Sites and Food Sources

The impact of deforestation on bird populations in India is profound, disrupting ecosystems and threatening numerous species. India's forests, from the Western Ghats to northeastern rainforests, are vital habitats for a diverse array of birds. However, rapid deforestation driven by human activities has led to widespread habitat loss, destroying nesting sites and food sources essential for bird survival. Nesting sites are critical for bird reproduction. Many species depend on specific trees or vegetation to build nests, raise young, and seek shelter. Deforestation has been particularly harmful to species reliant on mature forests. For instance, cavity-nesting birds like hornbills and woodpeckers face significant challenges as the trees they depend on are felled. Hornbills, needing large, old trees with cavities for nesting, struggle to find appropriate sites, leading to reduced breeding success and population declines.

Ground-nesting and shrub-nesting birds, such as the Indian pitta and various warblers, are also affected. They rely on dense undergrowth for nesting, which is often cleared for agriculture and development. The loss of these habitats reduces reproductive options and disrupts the ecosystem, as birds play crucial roles in seed dispersal, pollination, and pest control. Food sources for birds are tightly linked to forest health and diversity. Insects, fruits, seeds, and small vertebrates form the primary diet for many species. Deforestation disrupts these food chains by removing the vegetation that supports diverse insect populations. Insectivorous birds like flycatchers and warblers face significant food shortages due to the decline in insect populations. Similarly, fruit-eating birds such as barbets and pigeons suffer from the loss of fruit-bearing trees, forcing them to travel greater distances for food, increasing energy expenditure, and exposing them to higher predation risks.

The decline in bird populations also disrupts seed dispersal, crucial for forest regeneration. Many tropical trees rely on birds to spread their seeds, ensuring species survival and forest recovery. The reduction in bird populations thus hinders these mutualistic relationships, impeding forest regeneration and ecosystem stability.

2.2 Invasive Species: Competition and the Introduction of Diseases

The impact of deforestation on bird populations in India is profound, disrupting ecosystems and threatening numerous species. India's forests, from the Western Ghats to northeastern rainforests, are vital habitats for a diverse array of birds. However, rapid deforestation driven by human activities has led to widespread habitat loss, destroying nesting sites and food sources essential for bird survival. Nesting sites are critical for bird reproduction. Many species depend on specific trees or vegetation to build nests, raise young, and seek shelter. Deforestation has been particularly harmful to species reliant on mature forests. For instance, cavity-nesting birds like hornbills and woodpeckers face significant challenges as the trees they depend on are felled. Hornbills, needing large, old trees with cavities for nesting, struggle to find appropriate sites, leading to reduced breeding success and population declines.

Ground-nesting and shrub-nesting birds, such as the Indian pitta and various warblers, are also affected. They rely on dense undergrowth for nesting, which is often cleared for agriculture and development. The loss of these habitats reduces reproductive options and disrupts the ecosystem, as birds play crucial roles in seed dispersal, pollination, and pest control. Food sources for birds are tightly linked to forest health and diversity. Insects, fruits, seeds, and small vertebrates form the primary diet for many species. Deforestation disrupts these food chains by removing the vegetation that supports diverse insect populations. Insectivorous birds like flycatchers and warblers face significant food shortages due to the decline in insect populations. Similarly, fruit-eating birds such as barbets and pigeons suffer from the loss of fruit-bearing trees, forcing them to travel greater distances for food, increasing energy expenditure, and exposing them to higher predation risks.

The decline in bird populations also disrupts seed dispersal, crucial for forest regeneration. Many tropical trees rely on birds to spread their seeds, ensuring species survival and forest recovery. The reduction in bird populations thus hinders these mutualistic relationships, impeding forest regeneration and ecosystem stability.

3. Consequences of Fragmentation: Isolating Bird Populations

3.1 Reduced Genetic Diversity and Increased Vulnerability

Habitat fragmentation poses a significant threat to bird populations in India, leading to decreased genetic diversity and heightened vulnerability among avian species. This process occurs when large, continuous habitats are divided into smaller, isolated patches due to human activities such as deforestation, urbanization, and agriculture. These fragmented habitats not only reduce the overall suitable habitat area but also create physical barriers that impede bird movement between patches. The consequences are profound, impacting genetic health, reproductive success, and long-term survival. Genetic diversity is crucial for species' resilience to environmental changes and diseases. Fragmentation isolates bird populations, segregating their gene pools and diminishing genetic diversity. This isolation increases the likelihood of inbreeding, where closely related individuals mate, leading to inbreeding depression characterized by reduced fitness and reproductive success. For instance, fragmented populations of the endangered Great Indian Bustard exhibit lower genetic diversity and higher inbreeding rates, contributing to population decline.

Furthermore, isolated populations are vulnerable to genetic drift, where random changes in allele frequencies over time can lead to the loss of genetic variation and fixation of harmful alleles. This reduces their ability to adapt to environmental changes like climate fluctuations and habitat alterations. The Forest Owlet, endemic to central India and critically endangered, illustrates this vulnerability with its limited genetic diversity due to habitat fragmentation, hindering its adaptive potential. Fragmentation also disrupts gene flow between populations essential for maintaining genetic diversity and facilitating adaptation. Physical barriers like roads and urban areas hinder bird movement and interbreeding, exacerbating genetic isolation. For example, the Nilgiri Flycatcher in the Western Ghats faces significant barriers to gene flow due to fragmented habitats, compromising its resilience to environmental changes and increasing extinction risk.

Moreover, fragmentation affects social structures and breeding behaviors critical for reproductive success. For instance, the Lesser Florican in northwestern India has seen disruptions in cooperative breeding behavior due to fragmented grasslands, further threatening its survival. In addition to these biological impacts, fragmented habitats expose bird populations to environmental stochasticity, increasing vulnerability to unpredictable events like disease outbreaks or extreme weather. Smaller populations are particularly susceptible, as seen in the Indian Vulture, where reduced genetic diversity limits recovery from catastrophic events.

Lastly, edge effects at habitat boundaries exacerbate challenges by altering microclimates, increasing predation, and facilitating invasion by non-native species. Birds like the Malabar Trogon suffer as edge habitats diminish nesting and food resources, while also exposing them to heightened predation and competition.

3.1 Disrupted Connectivity and Hindered Migration Routes

Habitat fragmentation in India poses significant challenges for bird populations, affecting their connectivity and migration patterns crucial for survival and reproduction. As vast, continuous habitats are divided into smaller, isolated patches, birds encounter barriers that disrupt their movement and genetic exchange. This fragmentation alters behaviors, physiology, and population dynamics of both resident and migratory species. Connectivity between habitats is essential for accessing resources, finding mates, and maintaining genetic diversity through gene flow. Fragmentation, however, isolates populations, increasing their vulnerability to local extinctions. The Forest Owlet in central India exemplifies this, with its habitat fragmented into smaller patches that impede movement and gene flow, leading to isolated, at-risk populations.

Migratory birds, such as the Siberian Crane, face severe impacts as fragmentation disrupts critical stopover sites across their vast migration routes. Loss of wetlands in northern India, essential for resting and refueling, hampers their journey and threatens their survival. Similarly, the Indian Bustard contends with fragmented grasslands surrounded by inhospitable agricultural lands and infrastructure, risking collisions and hindering movement. Moreover, fragmented landscapes alter migration timings critical for successful reproduction. Birds like the Amur Falcon experience delays and mistimed arrivals at breeding grounds due to degraded stopover habitats along their routes, impacting reproductive success and offspring survival.

Changes in migration routes further exacerbate risks, forcing birds like the Black-tailed Godwit to traverse longer, more hazardous paths with fewer opportunities to refuel, impacting overall survival and breeding success. These disruptions extend beyond individual species, affecting entire bird communities and ecosystem functions such as seed dispersal and pest control. The decline of migratory species due to disrupted migration routes can disrupt ecological processes, altering plant communities and habitat structures, thereby affecting broader ecosystem health.

4. Habitat Restoration: Efforts to Reclaim Lost Paradise

4.1 Reforestation Initiatives and Creating Corridors

Reforestation initiatives and the creation of ecological corridors are pivotal strategies to restore habitats and support bird populations in India. These approaches counteract habitat loss and fragmentation, providing birds with the necessary resources and connectivity to thrive. Reforestation involves planting native tree species to restore degraded lands, while ecological corridors link fragmented habitats, allowing species to move freely. Both strategies are essential for maintaining biodiversity, enhancing ecosystem services, and ensuring the long-term survival of bird populations. Reforestation initiatives in India are diverse and widespread, targeting various ecosystems across the country. These efforts often involve the collaboration of government agencies, non-governmental organizations (NGOs), local communities, and international bodies. One notable example is the Green India Mission, launched by the Indian government in 2010 as part of the National Action Plan on Climate Change. This mission aims to increase forest and tree cover by 5 million hectares, improve the quality of existing forests, and enhance ecosystem services, including biodiversity conservation and water security. The mission focuses on restoring degraded forest lands, protecting biodiversity-rich areas, and involving local communities in the planning and implementation of reforestation activities.

Community involvement is critical for successful reforestation initiatives. Local communities possess valuable environmental knowledge and can significantly contribute to the selection of appropriate tree species, site preparation, planting, and maintenance. Engaging communities also ensures that reforestation efforts are sustainable and aligned with local needs and priorities. For instance, in Uttarakhand, the Van Panchayat system empowers local communities to manage forest resources and undertake reforestation activities. These community-managed forests provide habitat for birds and other wildlife while supporting livelihoods through sustainable harvesting of forest products.

Several NGOs are actively involved in reforestation efforts across India. Organizations like the Foundation for Ecological Security (FES) and the Wildlife Trust of India (WTI) work to restore degraded habitats, protect biodiversity, and promote sustainable land-use practices. FES, for instance, focuses on restoring common lands and pastures in rural areas, vital for both wildlife and local communities. By planting native tree species and implementing soil and water conservation measures, FES helps create resilient ecosystems that support diverse bird species, including the critically endangered Great Indian Bustard (Ardeotis nigriceps).

Creating ecological corridors is another essential strategy for restoring habitat connectivity and facilitating the movement of bird species. Corridors are continuous stretches of habitat that link fragmented landscapes, allowing species to move between patches for feeding, breeding, and dispersal. These corridors are particularly important for migratory birds, which rely on a network of habitats across their migration routes. In India, several initiatives are underway to establish and enhance ecological corridors.

One significant corridor project is the Western Ghats Biodiversity Hotspot, a mountain range parallel to India's western coast. The Western Ghats is one of the most biologically diverse regions in the world, home to numerous endemic and endangered bird species. However, habitat fragmentation due to deforestation, agriculture, and infrastructure development has threatened this biodiversity. Conservation organizations and government agencies are working together to create and restore corridors in the Western Ghats, ensuring connectivity between protected areas and other critical habitats. These efforts involve reforestation, habitat restoration, and establishing wildlife sanctuaries and community reserves.

Another important corridor initiative is the Kaziranga-Karbi Anglong Landscape in Assam, connecting Kaziranga National Park with the Karbi Anglong hills. Kaziranga is renowned for its rich biodiversity, including several endangered bird species such as the Bengal Florican (Houbaropsis bengalensis) and the White-bellied Heron (Ardea insignis). The Karbi Anglong hills provide a crucial habitat for these species, but deforestation and habitat degradation have created barriers to movement. The corridor project focuses on restoring degraded forests, reducing human-wildlife conflict, and engaging local communities in conservation efforts. Enhancing connectivity supports the long-term survival of bird populations and other wildlife in the region.

4.2 Importance of Community Involvement and Conservation Education

Community involvement and conservation education are pivotal in restoring bird habitats in India, forming the foundation for effective and sustainable conservation efforts. Engaging local communities ensures that conservation measures are culturally appropriate, ecologically sound, and economically beneficial. Concurrently, conservation education deepens understanding of biodiversity, instills stewardship, and empowers individuals to support conservation. Together, these strategies create a synergistic approach to address the complex challenges faced by bird populations in India.

Local communities, as primary stewards of natural resources, possess intricate knowledge of their environments. Their involvement in conservation projects is crucial. Firstly, community participation grounds conservation initiatives in local realities and traditions. Indigenous knowledge systems, developed over generations, offer valuable insights into sustainable resource management and ecological restoration. For instance, the Bishnoi community in Rajasthan has long practiced wildlife conservation and tree planting, guided by religious beliefs and customs, preserving critical habitats for various bird species. This exemplifies the effectiveness of community-led conservation.

Secondly, community involvement promotes the sustainability of conservation efforts by aligning them with local economic interests. Many Indian communities depend on natural resources for livelihoods, including agriculture, forestry, and fishing. Conservation initiatives that incorporate sustainable livelihood options can reduce pressure on natural habitats while benefiting local economies. Eco-tourism projects in regions like the Western Ghats and the Sundarbans combine habitat restoration with income generation. These projects create employment in guiding, hospitality, and handicrafts, incentivizing habitat protection and fostering community ownership.

Engaging local communities also enhances the social and political acceptability of conservation initiatives. When communities actively participate in planning and implementation, they are more likely to support and advocate for these efforts. This grassroots support is crucial for overcoming political and institutional barriers to conservation. The Joint Forest Management (JFM) program in India, involving local communities in forest resource management, has significantly improved forest cover and biodiversity. By fostering partnerships between government agencies and communities, the JFM program has created a more inclusive and participatory approach to conservation.

Conservation education is equally critical for effective habitat restoration. Education programs raising awareness about biodiversity and threats to bird populations can inspire action and support for conservation initiatives. These programs target diverse audiences, including school children, college students, local communities, policymakers, and the general public.In schools, integrating environmental education into the curriculum teaches students about biodiversity's value and conservation needs. Hands-on activities like birdwatching, tree planting, and nature walks help students connect with nature and foster a lifelong interest in conservation. For example, the Salim Ali Nature Clubs, established by the Bombay Natural History Society (BNHS), engage school children in birdwatching and nature study activities, promoting environmental awareness and conservation values from a young age.

DATA SHEET - IV
POLLUTION'S PERIL: A MULTIFACETED THREAT TO BIRDS

Study Title	Key Findings	Citation
Effect of air and noise pollution on species diversity and population at Lalpahari, West Bengal, India	Significant impact of air and noise pollution on species diversity and population of birds.	[44]
Air pollution and wildlife toxicology: An overlooked problem	Air pollution causes respiratory problems in birds, affecting their overall health.	[45]
Birds fall to earth from Delhi's toxic skies; these brothers are there to save them	Toxic air quality in Delhi leads to a high number of birds falling due to respiratory issues.	[46]

Stricken By Smog: Toxic Air Is Choking Birds Too	High pollution levels and winter conditions adversely affect birds' health.	[47]
Migratory birds missing as pollution levels rise in Delhi NCR	Rising pollution levels lead to a decrease in migratory birds visiting Delhi NCR.	[48]
Warning on nine pollutants and their effects on avian communities	Comprehensive review of the impact of various pollutants on birds.	[49]
Projected Shifts in Bird Distribution in India under Climate Change	Climate change, influenced by pollution, affects bird distribution in India.	[50]
10 Ways Air Pollution Impacts Birds: Understanding the Ecological Consequences	Various air pollutants cause respiratory problems and affect bird habitats.	[51]
Birds flee or die in polluted NCR	The study found that air pollution is causing birds to flee or die in the National Capital Region (NCR) of India. Up to 80% of birds brought to the author's attention were suffering from ailments caused by air pollution.	[52]
12 Unimaginable Effects of Air Pollution on Birds	This article discusses the various negative impacts of air pollution on birds, including reduced egg production, altered behavior, and increased mortality.	[53]
Impacts of Artificial Lighting on Avian Biodiversity: A Case Study of Udaipur (Rajasthan), India	The study found that excessive artificial lighting in Udaipur, India, significantly affects avian biodiversity, with higher diversity observed in darker areas compared to brighter areas.	[54]
Samachar: Print News Media on Air Pollution in India	The study analyzes the news media response to air pollution in India, revealing temporal and geographical biases in the coverage, as well as discrepancies between the sources discussed and the scientific evidence.	[55]

Spatial Variation of Trace Metals between Industrial and Rural Dwelling Birds of India	The study found higher concentrations of trace metals, such as chromium and copper, in the fecal pellets of blue rock pigeons in an industrial area compared to a rural area, indicating the impact of industrial pollution on avian species.	[56]
Air pollution is threatening birds' health	The article discusses how air pollution, particularly polycyclic aromatic hydrocarbons, can have negative impacts on birds, including reduced egg production and hatching, increased nest or brood abandonment, and reduced growth.	[57]
The impact of urbanisation on avian species: The inextricable link between people and birds	The study found that noise pollution can reduce species richness across different taxa, including birds, in urban areas.	[58]
Noise and light pollution affect breeding habits in birds	The article discusses how noise and light pollution can harm the health of bird populations by affecting their breeding habits.	[59]
Light pollution on the rise in India: Study	The article reports that light pollution is increasing in India, which can lead to disorientation and fatality for young turtles and birds.	[60]
Ruling the roost: Avian species reclaim urban habitat during India's COVID-19 lockdown	The study found that during the COVID-19 lockdown in India, urban avian species richness increased by 16%, likely due to a reduction in noise and air pollution.	[60]
A biogeographical description of the wild waterbird species associated with high-risk landscapes of Japanese encephalitis virus in India	The study identified 21 target waterbird species for Japanese encephalitis virus surveillance in India, highlighting the importance of incorporating wild reservoirs into disease monitoring efforts.	[61]

Impact of Chaotic Urbanisation on Bengaluru's (India) Urban Avian Diversity	The study found that urbanization is causing a decline in the number of avian species in Bengaluru, India, due to factors such as habitat loss and pollution.	[62]
Effects of ambient air pollution on respiratory health of adults: findings from a cross-sectional study in Chandrapur, Maharashtra, India	The study found that adults living in the industrial area of Chandrapur, Maharashtra, had a higher prevalence of respiratory symptoms, such as dry cough, sneezing, and asthma, compared to those living in the control area, indicating the impact of air pollution on human health.	[63]
Birds and pollution	The article discusses the various ways in which increasing human activity and pollution can affect birds, including through habitat degradation, bioaccumulation of toxic substances, and disruption of breeding and foraging behaviors.	[64]
Warning on nine Pollutants and their effects on avian communities	The study provides a comprehensive review of the potential impacts of various pollutants, including heavy metals, pesticides, and persistent organic pollutants, on avian communities.	[49]

CHAPTER 4

Pollution's Peril: A Multifaceted Threat

1. A Toxic Cocktail: Sources and Impacts of Pollution on Birds

1.1 Oil Spills and Industrial Waste: Direct Contamination and Habitat Degradation

Oil spills and industrial waste pose significant threats to avian populations and their habitats, resulting in direct contamination and severe habitat degradation. These pollutants primarily originate from human activities such as the extraction, transportation, and processing of petroleum products, as well as industrial operations that discharge hazardous waste into the environment. The ramifications for birds are extensive, impacting their physiology, behavior, reproductive success, and ultimately, their survival. Oil spills release large quantities of crude oil or refined petroleum products into marine and coastal environments, where their physical properties wreak havoc on birds. When oil coats a bird's feathers, it disrupts their natural waterproofing and insulation, leading to hypothermia due to impaired temperature regulation. The added weight and reduced buoyancy also hinder the birds' ability to fly, swim, and forage, increasing energy expenditure while reducing food intake.

The ingestion of oil during preening or while feeding on contaminated prey exacerbates the problem. Toxic compounds in the oil cause internal damage to the digestive tract, liver, and kidneys, leading to anemia, impaired immune function, and various physiological disorders. Long-term reproductive issues, such as reduced egg production, embryonic deformities, and lower hatching success rates, further threaten affected bird species. The Indian Skimmer (Rynchops albicollis) and various terns, which rely heavily on coastal and estuarine habitats, are particularly vulnerable to oil spill incidents. Industrial waste, including heavy metals and hazardous chemicals, is often released into water bodies, soil, and air as byproducts of manufacturing, mining, and other industrial processes. Heavy metals like lead, mercury, and cadmium are particularly concerning due to their toxicity and persistence. These contaminants accumulate in bird tissues, causing chronic health issues such as neurological damage, reproductive failure, and weakened immune systems.

Birds inhabiting or foraging in industrial areas or near contaminated water bodies face high exposure risks. Wetlands and rivers adjacent to industrial zones can become sinks for heavy metals and other pollutants, creating hazardous environments for waterfowl and other avian species. The bioaccumulation of these toxins in the food chain magnifies their impact, leading to secondary poisoning and population declines over time. Mercury pollution from coal-fired power plants and industrial processes exemplifies the detrimental effects of industrial waste. Mercury converts to methylmercury in aquatic environments, a highly toxic form that accumulates in fish and other aquatic organisms. Birds such as kingfishers, herons, and egrets, which prey on these organisms, are at significant risk of mercury poisoning, manifesting in impaired neurological function, reduced reproductive success, and death.

Beyond physiological impacts, oil spills and industrial waste cause extensive habitat degradation. Oil smothers coastal vegetation, such as mangroves and salt marshes, crucial for many birds species' survival. This habitat destruction forces birds to relocate to less suitable areas, increasing competition for resources and mortality rates. Industrial waste pollution alters water chemistry, contaminates soil, and destroys vegetation, with wetlands being particularly sensitive. Eutrophication from nutrient runoff leads to oxygen-depleted dead zones, diminishing food sources and making nesting sites unsuitable for birds.

1.2 Pesticides and Heavy Metals: Bioaccumulation and Reproductive Issues

Pesticides and heavy metals are among the most insidious pollutants affecting bird populations in India, stemming from agricultural practices, industrial processes, and various anthropogenic activities. These toxic substances have profound impacts on avian species, with bioaccumulation and reproductive issues being particularly concerning. Understanding the mechanisms of these pollutants and their effects on birds is crucial for developing effective conservation strategies and mitigating their harm. Pesticides, used primarily to protect crops from pests, have devastating non-target effects on birds. Commonly used pesticides such as organophosphates, carbamates, and neonicotinoids vary in their impact depending on chemical structure, environmental persistence, and exposure routes. Birds encounter pesticides through direct ingestion of treated seeds or crops, consumption of contaminated prey, inhalation of sprays, and skin absorption. Acute toxicity from these substances can lead to immediate health effects such as seizures, respiratory distress, and death. For instance, organophosphates inhibit acetylcholinesterase, causing severe neurological symptoms and rapid mortality in birds.

Chronic exposure to lower pesticide levels poses a more insidious threat. Over time, pesticides can bioaccumulate in bird tissues, leading to sub-lethal effects that impair health and reproductive success. Bioaccumulation occurs when birds repeatedly consume contaminated food or water, concentrating chemicals in their bodies. Persistent organic pollutants (POPs) are particularly concerning due to their resistance to degradation and prolonged environmental presence.

The organochlorine pesticide DDT (dichlorodiphenyltrichloroethane) exemplifies the dangers of pesticide bioaccumulation. Though banned in many countries, including India, DDT and its metabolites persist in ecosystems. DDT bioaccumulates in fatty tissues and biomagnifies up the food chain, resulting in high concentrations in top predators like raptors. This pesticide causes eggshell thinning, reducing reproductive success as fragile eggs break during incubation. The decline of species such as the Peregrine Falcon (Falco peregrinus) and the White-rumped Vulture (Gyps bengalensis) is linked to DDT exposure.

Neonicotinoids, a newer class of insecticides, also raise significant concerns. These systemic pesticides are absorbed by plants, present in pollen and nectar, and pose hazards to pollinators and birds. Studies indicate that neonicotinoids impair immune systems, reduce reproductive success, and alter feeding behaviors in birds. For instance, exposure to imidacloprid, a commonly used neonicotinoid, has been associated with reduced nestling growth and survival in seed-eating birds such as sparrows and finches.

2. Beyond the Obvious: Exploring Air and Electromagnetic Pollution

2.1 The Effects of Air Pollution: Reduced Visibility and Respiratory Issues

Air pollution poses a substantial threat to avian populations in India, manifesting in various deleterious effects on their health and survival. Among the many challenges presented by air pollution, reduced visibility and respiratory issues are particularly severe, influencing bird behavior, physiology, and ultimately, their survival rates. Reduced visibility due to air pollution primarily arises from the presence of particulate matter (PM) in the atmosphere. These fine particles, often emanating from vehicular emissions, industrial activities, and agricultural burning, create a dense smog that blankets large areas, especially in urban regions and during certain seasons. For birds, this reduced visibility can severely impair their ability to navigate, forage, and avoid predators. Many bird species rely heavily on their acute vision to locate food sources and to recognize and avoid threats. When visibility is compromised, birds may struggle to find sufficient food, leading to malnutrition and weakened immune systems. This is particularly critical for migratory birds that traverse long distances and depend on visual cues for navigation. The dense smog can disorient them, causing migratory disruptions, forcing birds to take longer, more arduous routes, or, in worst cases, leading to exhaustion and death.

In addition to navigation and foraging challenges, reduced visibility can also affect birds' mating and social behaviors. Many bird species use visual signals to attract mates and establish territories. When air pollution diminishes these visual cues, it can interfere with mating rituals and territory defense. For instance, the vibrant plumage of male birds, which is often used to attract females, may become less visible, reducing their chances of successful mating. Similarly, territorial disputes that rely on visual displays can become more frequent and prolonged, increasing the energy expenditure and stress levels in birds. Moreover, the inability to detect predators due to poor visibility can lead to increased predation rates. Birds that cannot see approaching predators in time may be caught off guard, leading to higher mortality rates. This not only affects individual birds but can also have cascading effects on bird populations, especially for species already vulnerable or with low reproductive rates.

Respiratory issues in birds caused by air pollution are another critical concern. Birds have highly efficient respiratory systems, which makes them particularly susceptible to airborne pollutants. The inhalation of fine particulate matter, sulfur dioxide, nitrogen oxides, and other toxic substances can cause a range of respiratory problems in birds, from mild irritation to severe respiratory diseases. Inhalation of these pollutants can lead to inflammation of the respiratory tract, reduced lung function, and increased susceptibility to infections. Particulate matter, especially PM2.5, can penetrate deep into the respiratory system, causing chronic respiratory diseases. Studies have shown that prolonged exposure to air pollution can lead to the development of conditions such as bronchitis, asthma-like symptoms, and other pulmonary issues in birds. These conditions can severely impair a bird's ability to breathe, reducing their overall fitness and ability to perform essential activities such as flying, foraging, and evading predators.

In addition to particulate matter, birds are also affected by gaseous pollutants such as sulfur dioxide (SO2) and nitrogen oxides (NOx). These gases can cause direct damage to the respiratory tissues, leading to chronic respiratory diseases. For instance, SO2, a common byproduct of fossil fuel combustion, can irritate the lining of the respiratory tract, causing inflammation and increased mucus production. This can lead to coughing, wheezing, and difficulty breathing, significantly affecting a bird's health and survival. The health impacts of air pollution on birds are not limited to respiratory issues alone. There is also evidence to suggest that air pollution can weaken the immune system, making birds more susceptible to infections and diseases. The inhalation of pollutants can cause oxidative stress, leading to the production of harmful free radicals that can damage cells and tissues. This oxidative stress can impair the immune system, reducing the bird's ability to fight off pathogens and increasing their vulnerability to diseases.

2.2 Electromagnetic Radiation: Potential Impacts on Bird Migration and Density

Electromagnetic radiation, a byproduct of our increasingly technological world, presents a significant yet often overlooked threat to avian populations, particularly impacting their migration patterns and population density. The rapid expansion of telecommunication networks, including mobile towers, Wi-Fi networks, and other sources of electromagnetic fields (EMFs), has created a pervasive environment that birds cannot escape. Understanding how this form of pollution affects avian life is crucial for developing strategies to mitigate its impact and preserve bird populations. Birds rely heavily on their natural ability to navigate using the Earth's magnetic field, a process known as magnetoreception. This biological compass is essential for migratory species, guiding them across vast distances to their breeding and wintering grounds. Electromagnetic radiation, especially from anthropogenic sources such as mobile phone towers and radar installations, has been shown to interfere with this magnetoreception. Studies demonstrate that exposure to electromagnetic fields can disrupt the magnetite-based receptors in birds, leading to disorientation and impaired navigation. This disruption can have severe consequences, as migratory birds may become lost, fail to reach their destinations, or expend excessive energy trying to correct their course. Such disorientation threatens individual birds and can lead to population declines if migratory routes are consistently disrupted.

The interference with magnetoreception is particularly concerning for species that undertake long migratory journeys, such as the bar-headed goose, which crosses the Himalayas, and the Amur falcon, which travels from Siberia to Southern Africa. These species rely on precise navigation to survive their arduous journeys. When electromagnetic radiation disturbs their ability to navigate accurately, they may end up in unsuitable habitats where food and shelter are scarce, leading to increased mortality rates. Furthermore, disoriented birds are more vulnerable to predation and adverse weather conditions, exacerbating the risks associated with disrupted migration.

In addition to affecting navigation, electromagnetic radiation can impact bird behavior in more subtle ways. For instance, birds use the Earth's magnetic field to orient themselves during daily activities such as foraging and roosting. Electromagnetic interference can lead to confusion and stress, disrupting these essential behaviors. Birds that are unable to effectively locate food or safe resting places may experience increased stress levels, reduced body condition, and lower reproductive success. Over time, these behavioral disruptions can contribute to population declines, particularly in areas with high levels of electromagnetic pollution.

Moreover, electromagnetic radiation has been linked to changes in bird density and distribution. Some studies have found that birds tend to avoid areas with high levels of electromagnetic pollution, leading to changes in their distribution patterns. This avoidance behavior can result in the fragmentation of habitats, as birds are forced to relocate to less suitable areas. Habitat fragmentation is a significant concern for many bird species, as it can lead to smaller, isolated populations that are more vulnerable to genetic bottlenecks, reduced genetic diversity, and increased risk of local extinction. Additionally, the displacement of birds from high-quality habitats can increase competition for resources in less suitable areas, further stressing bird populations.

3. Water Pollution's Devastating Impact

3.1 Contamination of Waterways and Loss of Prey Species

Water pollution poses an escalating threat to bird populations in India, intricately linked to industrial discharges, agricultural runoff, domestic waste, and plastic pollution. These pollutants collectively create a toxic environment, significantly undermining avian health and survival. Industrial activities in India discharge pollutants directly into rivers, lakes, and coastal areas, introducing heavy metals such as mercury, lead, and cadmium, alongside toxic chemicals like pesticides and pharmaceuticals into aquatic ecosystems. Birds such as herons, kingfishers, and egrets, which rely on clean water bodies for fishing, face direct exposure to these contaminants. The bioaccumulation of heavy metals in their bodies can lead to severe poisoning, resulting in neurological damage, impaired reproduction, and mortality. For instance, mercury, a potent neurotoxin, disrupts the central nervous system of birds, causing behavioral changes, reduced motor function, and impaired hunting abilities.

Agricultural runoff significantly contributes to water pollution, affecting bird populations through the leaching of chemical fertilizers and pesticides into nearby water bodies. Fertilizer-induced nutrient pollution causes eutrophication, resulting in excessive algal growth that depletes oxygen levels, creating hypoxic conditions detrimental to aquatic life. Birds feeding on fish and other aquatic organisms suffer as declining oxygen levels lead to massive fish kills and disrupted food webs. Additionally, pesticides directly poison birds through ingestion of contaminated water or prey, causing acute toxicity, reproductive failures, and weakened immune systems.

Domestic waste, especially untreated sewage, heavily contaminates Indian waterways. The discharge of human waste and household chemicals into rivers and lakes introduces pathogens, organic matter, and pollutants into aquatic environments. Birds that contact or consume contaminated water risk contracting diseases, while high levels of organic pollutants promote harmful bacterial and viral proliferation. Waterborne pathogens can cause gastrointestinal diseases in birds, leading to dehydration, malnutrition, and increased mortality. Furthermore, organic matter accumulation exacerbates eutrophication, compounding negative impacts on aquatic ecosystems and bird populations.

Plastic pollution represents an emerging and visible threat to bird species in India. Rivers and coastal areas are littered with plastic debris, from large items like bottles and bags to microplastics. Birds foraging along polluted waterways ingest plastic pieces, mistaking them for food. Ingested plastics cause internal injuries, digestive tract blockages, and starvation, as birds cannot digest or excrete the foreign materials. Plastics also absorb and concentrate toxic chemicals from surrounding water, leading to secondary poisoning when birds consume contaminated particles. The ingestion of plastics compromises bird health and reproductive success, potentially causing broader population declines.

The loss of prey species due to water pollution further threatens bird populations. Aquatic insects, fish, amphibians, and small organisms constitute the primary diet for many bird species. Polluted water bodies lead to high mortality rates and population declines of these prey species. For instance, amphibians like frogs, highly sensitive to pollutants, suffer developmental abnormalities, reproductive failures, and increased disease susceptibility in contaminated waters. As prey populations decline, birds relying on these food sources face malnutrition and reduced breeding success, exacerbating the threat of water pollution to avian populations in India.

3.2 Oil Spills: Damaging Feathers and Leading to Hypothermia

Oil spills present a severe and multifaceted threat to bird populations in India, particularly affecting coastal and marine species. These environmental disasters can cause catastrophic damage to bird feathers, leading to hypothermia, loss of buoyancy, and impaired flight. The impact of oil spills on birds extends beyond immediate physical harm, affecting their behavior, reproductive success, and long-term survival. Understanding the mechanisms through which oil spills harm birds and the broader ecological consequences is essential for developing effective response strategies and conservation efforts.

When oil spills occur, the immediate concern for birds is the contamination of their feathers. Feathers are crucial for insulation, waterproofing, and flight. They have a complex structure that traps air, providing thermal insulation and enabling birds to maintain their body temperature even in cold water. Oil disrupts this delicate structure by coating the feathers and causing them to mat together. This not only compromises the insulation properties but also makes the feathers heavy and sticky, leading to a loss of buoyancy. Birds that rely on buoyancy to float on water, such as ducks, grebes, and cormorants, find it increasingly difficult to stay afloat when their feathers are coated with oil. As a result, they expend more energy to stay on the surface, leading to exhaustion and increased vulnerability to predators.

Hypothermia is one of the most immediate and severe consequences of oiling. Birds maintain their body temperature through the insulating properties of their feathers. When oil coats their feathers, it destroys the insulation, allowing cold water to reach the skin. Hypothermia can set in rapidly, especially in colder waters, as the bird's body loses heat faster than it can generate. Hypothermic birds become lethargic, making them less able to forage for food and evade predators. Prolonged exposure to hypothermic conditions can be fatal, as the bird's metabolic rate drops, and vital bodily functions slow down or cease altogether. In addition to immediate mortality, hypothermia weakens birds, making them more susceptible to secondary infections and diseases, further reducing their chances of survival.

Oil ingestion is another critical issue for birds affected by spills. In an attempt to clean their feathers, birds often ingest oil, which can have toxic effects on their internal organs. The ingestion of oil can lead to gastrointestinal issues, liver and kidney damage, and compromised immune function. Oil-coated prey also poses a risk, as birds consuming contaminated fish or invertebrates ingest the toxins present in the oil. The accumulation of these toxins can cause long-term health problems, including reproductive failures, reduced hatchability of eggs, and developmental defects in chicks. For example, polycyclic aromatic hydrocarbons (PAHs), which are common components of crude oil, are known to be carcinogenic and can cause mutations and cancers in birds.

The behavioral impact of oil spills on birds is profound. Oiled birds exhibit altered behaviors that affect their ability to feed, mate, and care for their young. Birds coated with oil spend more time preening in an attempt to clean their feathers, reducing the time available for foraging and other essential activities. This increased preening effort also means higher energy expenditure, which is particularly detrimental when food intake is compromised due to the bird's inability to hunt effectively. Additionally, oil exposure can impair the bird's sense of smell and taste, making it difficult to locate and identify food. For species that rely heavily on these senses for foraging, such as seabirds that detect fish schools by scent, oil contamination can lead to starvation and malnutrition.

Reproductive success is severely impacted by oil spills. Birds that are exposed to oil may experience reduced fertility and lower hatching success. Contaminants in the oil can lead to thinner eggshells, reducing the likelihood of successful incubation and hatching. Chicks that do hatch are often weak and have lower survival rates due to the compromised health of the parents and the toxic environment. Parental care is also disrupted, as oiled birds may abandon their nests or fail to provide adequate food and protection to their offspring. The cumulative effect of these factors can lead to significant population declines, particularly in species that are already threatened or have low reproductive rates.

4. The Effects of Light Pollution

4.1 Disrupting Migration Patterns and Mating Behavior

Light pollution, a pervasive consequence of urbanization and industrialization, significantly affects bird populations by disrupting migration patterns and mating behaviors. The omnipresence of artificial light at night (ALAN) alters the natural day-night cycle, leading to substantial ecological and behavioral changes in avian species. Understanding these impacts is crucial for developing strategies to mitigate the effects of light pollution and preserve bird biodiversity. Migratory birds heavily rely on natural light cues to navigate during their long journeys between breeding and wintering grounds. These cues include the position of the sun, moon, and stars, as well as the polarization of sunlight at twilight. Artificial lighting disrupts these natural navigational aids, causing disorientation and deviation from migratory routes. Birds attracted to brightly lit areas can become trapped in urban environments, expending energy in confusion and ultimately facing exhaustion. This phenomenon, known as "light trapping," leads to increased mortality rates as birds collide with buildings, towers, and other structures. Nocturnal migrants such as warblers, thrushes, and sparrows are particularly susceptible to light-induced disorientation, resulting in fatal collisions with illuminated skyscrapers and communication towers.

Furthermore, light pollution artificially extends day length, impacting the internal circadian rhythms of birds. These rhythms regulate various physiological and behavioral processes, including migration timing. Birds use the length of daylight, or photoperiod, to time their migratory departures. Artificial light can cause birds to misinterpret the season, leading to premature or delayed migrations. Early departure exposes birds to harsh climatic conditions, lack of food resources, and increased predation risks. Conversely, delayed migration can result in missed breeding opportunities, competition for resources, and arrival at wintering grounds after optimal conditions have passed. Species like the Asian koel and the pied cuckoo, which undertake seasonal migrations, face significant threats from disrupted migration timings due to light pollution.

Light pollution also affects the energetic balance and survival of migratory birds. Birds migrate to take advantage of seasonal food abundance and suitable breeding conditions. However, the energy costs of migration are high, and birds must arrive at their destinations with sufficient energy reserves for reproductive activities. Disorientation and extended travel times due to light pollution can deplete these reserves, reducing birds' physical condition upon arrival. This can lead to lower reproductive success, as weakened birds may be less capable of defending territories, attracting mates, or successfully raising offspring. The cumulative effect of repeated disruptions across generations can lead to population declines, particularly in long-distance migratory species.

Mating behavior is another critical aspect of bird life significantly influenced by light pollution. Many bird species rely on vocalizations and visual displays to attract mates, establish territories, and ward off rivals. These behaviors are often timed to occur during specific periods of the day or night, guided by natural light conditions. Artificial light can extend or shift these periods, leading to altered mating behaviors. Birds like the Indian robin and the oriental magpie-robin, which sing to attract mates, may begin their dawn chorus earlier or continue singing later into the evening under artificial light conditions. This can disrupt the synchronization of mating behaviors within populations, leading to reduced mating success and reproductive output.

Moreover, light pollution can affect the hormonal regulation of reproductive cycles in birds. Melatonin production, which regulates sleep and reproductive cycles, is influenced by light exposure. Artificial lighting can suppress melatonin production, leading to changes in the timing of breeding activities. Birds exposed to prolonged artificial light may experience earlier onset of breeding, leading to mismatched timing with peak food availability for raising chicks. This phenological mismatch can result in higher chick mortality rates due to inadequate food supply. Species such as the house sparrow and the common myna, which breed in urban environments, are particularly vulnerable to these hormonal disruptions caused by light pollution.

DATA SHEET - V
IMPACT OF CLIMATE CHANGE ON AVIAN SPECIES IN INDIA

Study Title	Key Findings	Citation
Migratory Birds in Peril: Unravelling the Impact of Climate Change	Avian migration crucial for survival is threatened by habitat loss and altered ecosystems due to climate change.	[65]
Effects of climate change on global biodiversity: a review of key literature	Examines impacts of climate change on tropical forest ecosystems and their biodiversity.	[66]
Impact of climate change on bird ecology, breeding seasonality, abundance, and distribution in Sikkim, India	Certain bird species in Sikkim are breeding later due to climate changes affecting their ecology and distribution.	[66]

Impact of chaotic urbanisation on Bengaluru's (India) urban avian diversity	Urban warming and habitat changes lead to reduced bird diversity in Bengaluru, affecting species dependent on specific ecosystems.	[62]
Interactive impacts of climate change and land-use	Apparent survival trends of 15 bird species show impacts of endemic biodiversity changes in the Indian Himalaya due to climate change and land-use changes.	[67]
The effects of climate change on global wildlife and terrestrial ecosystems	Climate change has the potential to alter demographic patterns and survival rates in avian species, leading to significant biodiversity changes.	[68]
The effects of weather on avian growth and implications for adaptation to climate change	Avian growth patterns affected by weather changes impact fledgling survival and recruitment, altering responses to climate change.	[69]
Markers for global climate change and its impact on social, biological and ecological systems: A review	Climate change shifts the distribution of grassland bird species, affecting both local and global ecosystems.	[69]
Climate change and its impact on Australia's avifauna	Indirect impacts of climate change on bird species due to altered habitats and ecosystems in the Indian Ocean region.	[70]
Birds and climate change: impacts and conservation responses	Documents the impact of climate change on bird species in southern India and China, highlighting conservation needs.	[71]
Climate change and its impact on terrestrial ecosystems	Examines the impact of climate change on avian species' tolerance levels and survival responses.	[72]
Ecological impacts of poultry waste on urban raptors: conflicts, diseases, and climate change implications amidst pandemic threats	Examines how poultry waste impacts urban raptors and their ecosystems, with implications for climate change.	[73]

Global impacts of climate change on avian functional diversity	Climate change impacts dispersal distance and survival of juvenile plants, affecting vegetation structure and avian diversity.	[74]
Climate change shifts the habitat suitability of range-restricted bird species (Catreus wallichii) in the Himalayan ecosystem	Observes habitat suitability changes for birds in the Himalayan ecosystem due to climate change.	[75]
The impacts of climate change on the annual cycles of birds	Highlights the impact of climate change on migration and reproduction cycles of birds.	[76]
Which traits influence bird survival in the city? A review	Investigates bird survival traits in urban environments affected by climate change.	[77]
Agricultural intensification, rainfall patterns, and large waterbird breeding success in the extensively cultivated landscape of Uttar Pradesh, India	Examines how agriculture and climate change impact waterbird breeding success.	[78]
Climate change impacts on Himalayan biodiversity: evidence-based perception and current approaches to evaluate threats under climate change	Reviews threats to Himalayan biodiversity from climate change, including avian malaria.	[79]
Ecology and evolution of avian malaria: implications of land use changes and climate change on disease dynamics	Analyzes how climate change and land-use changes impact avian malaria, influencing bird survival and ecosystem health.	[80]
Abiotic niche predictors of long-term trends in body mass and survival of Eastern Himalayan birds	Studies the synergistic impacts of climate change and habitat alterations on Eastern Himalayan birds, focusing on body mass and survival.	[81]

CHAPTER 5

Climate Change: Altered Ecosystems Impact on Avian Survival

1. Rising Temperatures: A Feverish Threat to Bird Habitats

1.1   Disrupted Breeding Cycles: Mismatches and Population Decline

The intricate relationship between climate change and avian breeding cycles in India reveals a complex web of disruptions, leading to population decline and ecological imbalance. Rising global temperatures alter seasonal patterns, affecting bird breeding cycles which are closely synchronized with environmental cues such as temperature, precipitation, and food availability. These cues ensure breeding occurs when resources are plentiful, maximizing offspring survival. However, climate change shifts these cues, causing mismatches between breeding timing and resource availability.

Many bird species cue their breeding to increasing spring temperatures and longer daylight hours. However, with climate change, spring arrives earlier in India, prompting some birds to breed prematurely. This shift can cause a mismatch between the peak availability of food resources, such as insects or fruits, and the period when chicks need the most nourishment. Insect populations, crucial for feeding young birds, are driven by temperature and plant phenology. If insects emerge earlier due to warmer temperatures but birds do not adjust their breeding times, chicks may hatch when food is scarce, leading to higher mortality rates and reduced reproductive success.

Several Indian bird species illustrate this phenomenon. The Indian pitta, a migratory bird, traditionally breeds during the monsoon when insect abundance provides ample food for its chicks. However, changing rainfall patterns and rising temperatures make the monsoon timing unpredictable, causing pittas to breed too early or late, missing peak insect season and resulting in fewer chicks reaching maturity. Similarly, the Indian roller, which times its breeding with the availability of small reptiles and insects, faces disrupted synchronization due to erratic weather and fluctuating temperatures, impacting chick survival and overall population dynamics. Climate change-induced habitat alterations further exacerbate these mismatches. Many bird species depend on specific habitats for breeding. For instance, the endangered Great Indian Bustard relies on grasslands for nesting. Rising temperatures and changing precipitation patterns are transforming these grasslands, making them less suitable for breeding, thus contributing to the bustard's declining population. The impact of disrupted breeding cycles extends beyond individual species to entire ecosystems. Birds play crucial roles in their habitats, such as pollination, seed dispersal, and pest control. Declining bird populations due to breeding mismatches compromise these ecosystem services, leading to broader ecological consequences.

1.2 Altered Rainfall Patterns: Reduced Food Availability and Habitat Loss

The profound impact of altered rainfall patterns on avian species in India is multifaceted, influencing food availability, habitat quality, and overall survival. Climate change has precipitated significant shifts in precipitation patterns, resulting in more erratic and unpredictable rainfall. These changes have far-reaching consequences for bird populations, particularly in terms of food availability and habitat loss. Birds rely heavily on stable environmental conditions for their survival, and any disruption can have cascading effects on their populations and the ecosystems they inhabit.

Rainfall patterns critically determine the availability of food resources for birds. Many species time their breeding and migration cycles to coincide with periods of peak food abundance, often linked to seasonal rains. However, climate change has rendered these patterns increasingly irregular. For instance, the Indian monsoon, a key determinant of regional rainfall, has shown signs of delayed onset and premature withdrawal. Such shifts can lead to prolonged dry spells or sudden, intense rain events, both of which disrupt food availability for birds.

The effects of altered rainfall patterns are evident in the breeding success of many bird species. Insectivorous birds, which rely on insect emergence post-rains, are particularly vulnerable. The Indian Pitta, a migratory species breeding during the monsoon, is directly influenced by the timing and intensity of these rains. Delays or insufficiencies in rainfall result in scarce insect populations, leading to poor chick survival and reduced reproductive success.

Similarly, frugivorous birds, dependent on fruit-bearing trees, suffer from disrupted fruiting cycles due to erratic rainfall. For example, the Malabar Pied Hornbill relies on consistent rainfall for the fruiting of key trees. Erratic rainfall patterns affect these cycles, reducing food availability and impacting forest regeneration and ecosystem health due to decreased seed dispersal by these birds.

Waterbirds and wetland-dependent species are also severely impacted by altered rainfall patterns. Wetlands, crucial breeding and feeding habitats, are highly sensitive to changes in precipitation. Reduced rainfall can dry up wetlands, while excessive rainfall can cause flooding, both of which render these habitats unsuitable. The Sarus Crane, an iconic wetland species, has seen declining populations due to habitat loss from changing rainfall patterns. These cranes require shallow wetlands for nesting and feeding, and any alteration in water levels affects their breeding success and chick survival.

Moreover, changing rainfall patterns exacerbate habitat degradation. Forests, grasslands, and wetlands are all affected by shifts in precipitation, leading to habitat loss and fragmentation. In forests, prolonged dry periods increase wildfire risk, destroying nesting sites and food sources. Grasslands, home to species like the Great

Indian Bustard, rely on a delicate balance of wet and dry periods, with disruptions leading to unsuitable conditions for nesting and foraging.

The impact extends beyond direct effects on food and habitat. Altered rainfall influences bird behavior and physiology, with stress from unpredictable resources affecting health and reproductive success. Studies show that food scarcity due to altered rainfall leads to reduced body condition, lower immune function, and higher stress hormone levels, contributing to population declines.

Migration patterns are also disrupted. Many migratory species rely on rainfall cues to time migrations. Changes in these cues can cause mistimed migrations, leading birds to arrive at breeding or wintering grounds either too early or too late. The Bar-headed Goose, migrating to India from Central Asia, is one example. Arriving too early due to altered rainfall can result in unsuitable conditions and insufficient food, impacting survival and fitness.

The ripple effects of altered rainfall extend to entire ecosystems. Birds play crucial roles in pollination, seed dispersal, and pest control. Declines in bird populations due to rainfall changes compromise these ecosystem services, affecting plant reproduction, pest populations, agriculture, and human livelihoods.

2. Shifting Distribution Ranges: A Scramble for Survival

2.1 Limited Suitable Habitat: Forced Migration and Competition for Resources

Climate change has profoundly altered the distribution ranges of bird species across India, presenting immediate and long-term challenges for avian populations. As temperatures rise and precipitation patterns shift, birds are compelled to migrate to new areas in search of suitable habitats. This forced migration is complex and fraught with difficulties, including the availability of suitable habitats and increased competition for limited resources.

For many species, the journey to new habitats is perilous. Birds that are traditionally sedentary or have limited migratory ranges face significant challenges. The inability to travel long distances or adapt quickly to new environments can lead to high mortality rates. For instance, the Indian Peafowl, primarily found in semi-arid regions, might struggle to find new habitats as their current ones become too hot or dry. The peafowl, revered and protected in many regions, might not find the same protection and suitable conditions elsewhere, potentially leading to population declines.

In addition to migration challenges, birds face intense competition for resources in their new habitats. As more species are forced to move, ecological niches become increasingly crowded. Birds must compete for food, nesting sites, and other vital resources with both resident species and other newcomers. This competition can be particularly fierce if the new habitat has limited resources to begin with. For example, wetlands, critical for many bird species, are shrinking due to climate change and human encroachment. Migratory waterfowl, such as the Northern Pintail, might find these wetlands unable to support their populations, leading to increased competition and stress on resident species like the Indian Spot-billed Duck.

Moreover, many areas are becoming ecological traps-regions where conditions appear suitable for birds but are actually suboptimal or dangerous. Agricultural fields, for instance, might attract birds due to the abundance of food in the form of crops, but these areas often come with risks such as pesticide exposure and human-wildlife conflict. Birds that migrate to these seemingly attractive habitats might suffer high mortality rates, thereby reducing the overall viability of their populations.

Climate change also affects the phenology of plants and the availability of insects, influencing bird migration and settlement patterns. Birds that migrate based on temperature cues might arrive at their new habitats before local food sources are available, leading to starvation and decreased reproductive success. The timing mismatch between the arrival of insectivorous birds and the peak availability of insects is a growing concern. For instance, the Pied Cuckoo, which migrates to India from Africa, might face challenges if the monsoon rains that trigger insect emergence are delayed or insufficient.

2.2 Vulnerability of Endemic Species: Restricted Ranges and Increased Extinction Risk

The susceptibility of endemic bird species to climate change in India poses a critical threat, driven by their restricted distributions and heightened risk of extinction. Endemic species, confined to specific geographic areas, face acute vulnerability as they often possess specialized habitat requirements and limited migratory capacities. The ongoing alterations in climate are increasingly jeopardizing their survival, necessitating urgent conservation interventions to safeguard their persistence.

India hosts several endemic bird species, such as the Nilgiri Laughingthrush, Malabar Parakeet, and Western Ghats' Sholakili, each adapted to distinct climatic and ecological niches. These birds thrive in biodiversity hotspots like the Western Ghats and the Eastern Himalayas, where they rely on region-specific habitats and resources. However, climate change is reshaping these environments through shifts in temperature and precipitation patterns, profoundly impacting the availability and suitability of their habitats. The specialized nature of endemic species limits their ability to adapt swiftly to such rapid environmental changes, escalating their susceptibility to habitat degradation and potential extinction.

A primary concern for endemic birds is the displacement of suitable habitats due to climate-induced alterations. Rising temperatures compel many species to seek cooler environments at higher altitudes or latitudes, mirroring their original habitats. However, this mobility is constrained for species like the Nilgiri Laughingthrush, confined to the shola-grassland ecosystems of the Nilgiri Hills, where higher elevations may not offer adequate habitat. This geographic restriction significantly heightens their risk of extinction.

Moreover, climate change disrupts the phenology of plants and availability of food resources critical for endemic bird survival. Many species have co-evolved with specific plant or insect species that constitute their diet. Variations in the timing of flowering, fruiting, and insect emergence due to climate change can lead to food shortages during crucial life stages such as breeding and chick-rearing. The White-bellied Blue Flycatcher, endemic to the Western Ghats, relies heavily on consistent insect populations for nurturing its offspring, thereby facing heightened vulnerability to disruptions in food availability.

Habitat fragmentation, exacerbated by climate change, poses another significant threat to endemic bird species. Fragmented habitats, influenced by human activities such as agriculture and urbanization, struggle to support viable bird populations over time. Despite being a continuous mountain range, the Western Ghats suffer from fragmentation, hindering the movement of species like the Malabar Parakeet and limiting their ability to locate new suitable habitats amidst environmental shifts.

3. The Plight of Migratory Birds: Facing Double Jeopardy

3.1 Disrupted Migration Routes: Uncertain Journeys and Increased Mortality

Migratory birds, celebrated for their remarkable journeys spanning continents, confront unprecedented challenges in the era of climate change. Disrupted migration routes introduce heightened uncertainty and peril, contributing to escalated mortality rates among these avian travelers. As global climate patterns continue to shift, the intricate equilibrium upon which migratory birds rely for survival faces profound disruption, echoing throughout ecosystems. Migration among birds represents an intricate dance evolved over millennia, finely attuned to synchronize with seasonal shifts and resource availability. These journeys span vast distances between breeding and wintering grounds, guided by precise environmental cues. However, climate change disrupts these cues, altering temperature regimes, precipitation patterns, and wind currents. Consequently, traditional migration paths become increasingly unpredictable, compelling birds to adjust their routes in response.

A critical consequence of climate change on migratory birds manifests through shifts in phenological signals that govern migration timing. Many species rely on cues like temperature and daylight duration to initiate their journeys. With rising global temperatures, these cues undergo shifts, prompting birds to commence migrations earlier or later than customary. Such mistiming can lead to severe repercussions; premature arrivals may encounter adverse weather conditions and food scarcity, while delayed arrivals risk missing peak resource availability critical for successful reproduction. Moreover, alterations in wind patterns due to climate change impose additional challenges on migratory journeys. Essential tailwinds that aid energy conservation during flights become less reliable, while opposing headwinds increase travel duration and energy expenditure. For species like the Bar-headed Goose, which undertakes arduous high-altitude flights across the Himalayas, these changes heighten the risk of fatigue and mortality, underscoring the vulnerability of migratory birds to climatic shifts.

The intensification of extreme weather events, such as storms and heatwaves, emerges as another formidable threat to migratory birds. More frequent and severe climatic disturbances disrupt migration patterns, potentially causing birds to veer off-course or encounter inhospitable conditions. Such events can result in heightened mortality rates as birds struggle to find suitable habitats for rest, foraging, and refuge. The Amur Falcon, navigating from Siberia to India, exemplifies the peril faced during migration through regions prone to severe weather impacts.

Furthermore, climate change imperils the availability of vital stopover sites crucial for refueling during long migrations. Wetlands, forests, and grasslands that serve as essential habitats are increasingly altered or lost due to climate variability and human activities. The depletion of these habitats diminishes opportunities for birds to rest and replenish energy reserves, potentially leading to starvation and reduced survival rates during migration. Species like the Common Crane, reliant on Indian wetlands and agricultural fields for pit stops, confront dwindling resources critical to successful migration.

3.2 Mismatches Between Breeding Timing and Food Availability: Unsynchronized Cycles

The synchronization of breeding timing with food availability is crucial for the survival of migratory birds, a balance increasingly disrupted by climate change. Species like the Pied Flycatcher, European Starling, and Eurasian Blackcap have evolved to coordinate their reproductive cycles with seasonal peaks in food resources, such as insects. This synchronization ensures adequate nourishment for both adults and their offspring during the demanding breeding season. However, rising temperatures and altered precipitation patterns are advancing the timing of plant growth and insect emergence, causing food peaks to occur earlier.

Migratory birds, unable to adjust their schedules as rapidly, often arrive at breeding grounds to find diminished food availability, particularly impacting species with fixed migration and breeding schedules like the European Starling. These mismatches threaten reproductive success, exemplified by observations of the Pied Flycatcher arriving in India to find declining caterpillar numbers, impacting chick survival. While some species, such as the Eurasian Blackcap, exhibit more flexibility in adjusting breeding timing, the broader trend highlights significant challenges posed by climate change to the survival strategies of migratory birds worldwide.

4. The Domino Effect: Climate Change and Cascading Impacts

4.1 Increased Frequency of Extreme Weather Events: Habitat Destruction and Displacement

In India, the escalating frequency and severity of extreme weather events, exacerbated by climate change, pose profound threats to avian populations across diverse habitats. From the towering Himalayas to the sprawling coastal mangroves, these regions harbor a rich tapestry of bird species, each intricately linked to specific ecological niches. However, the intensification of weather extremes-cyclones, heavy rainfall, droughts, and heatwaves-has triggered widespread habitat destruction and displacement, imperiling avian survival. Cyclones, increasingly frequent and severe along coastal areas, exact a devastating toll on avian habitats. Mangroves, critical breeding and feeding grounds for numerous bird species, are especially vulnerable.

Cyclonic winds ravage these forests, uprooting trees and disrupting the intricate ecosystem that birds depend upon. The aftermath sees widespread bird fatalities due to habitat loss, nesting site destruction, and the decimation of food sources, forcing survivors into less suitable environments with diminished prospects for survival. Heatwaves, escalating in frequency and intensity, exacerbate these challenges. Birds, reliant on evaporative cooling through water sources, suffer dehydration and heat stress as water supplies dwindle during heatwaves. Altered activity patterns to seek shade reduce foraging time, impacting health and reproductive success. Urban migration amid habitat loss introduces new risks, including collisions with structures, pollution exposure, and predation by domestic animals, further imperiling already stressed bird populations. The displacement of birds into agricultural and urban landscapes amidst habitat loss often sparks conflicts with human activities. Crop damage prompts defensive measures by farmers, escalating human-wildlife conflicts. Meanwhile, the ecological repercussions of habitat destruction extend beyond immediate losses, disrupting entire ecosystems reliant on these habitats. Mangroves, for instance, crucial for coastal resilience against storms, safeguard both wildlife and human communities, illustrating the interconnected impacts of habitat loss on broader ecological stability.

4.2 Sea Level Rise and Coastal Erosion: Loss of Breeding Grounds and Wetland Habitats

Sea level rise and coastal erosion, driven by climate change, profoundly impact avian populations in India, particularly through the loss of breeding grounds and wetland habitats. India's extensive coastline hosts diverse ecosystems such as mangroves, salt marshes, estuaries, and mudflats, crucial for resident and migratory bird species alike. However, accelerating sea level rise and coastal erosion pose significant threats, jeopardizing these habitats and thereby avian survival. Sea level rise leads to the inundation of low-lying coastal areas, submerging crucial breeding and foraging sites. Mangrove forests, essential for species like the mangrove whistler and lesser adjutant stork, face drowning of roots, causing habitat loss. Coastal erosion compounds these impacts by reducing available nesting and feeding grounds, particularly affecting birds reliant on sandy beaches, such as the Indian skimmer and various terns, whose colonies can be washed away by rising seas.

Wetlands like salt marshes and estuarine mudflats suffer as sea levels increase, altering their delicate saline balance and threatening species like the black-tailed godwit and curlew sandpiper, which depend on these areas during migratory stopovers. The decline in suitable habitats disrupts ecological functions such as seed dispersal, affecting mangrove regeneration and exacerbating erosion. Increased competition for resources in new territories further stresses displaced bird populations, impacting their reproductive success and mortality rates. Human activities exacerbate these challenges through coastal development that disrupts natural habitat migration and pollution that degrades water quality in coastal and wetland areas. Conservation efforts are vital, focusing on habitat restoration and protection. Projects like mangrove replanting and artificial reef construction help stabilize coastlines and provide refuge for birds. Buffer zones restricting coastal development allow habitats to migrate inland naturally, while managing water quality and hydrology supports wetland resilience.

5. Adaptation and Conservation: Strategies for a Changing Climate

5.1 Protected Areas and Habitat Corridors: Providing Refuge and Connectivity

In response to rapidly shifting climatic conditions, the establishment and maintenance of protected areas and habitat corridors have emerged as critical strategies for safeguarding avian species in India. Protected areas, including national parks, wildlife sanctuaries, and bird reserves, serve as essential sanctuaries where birds find refuge from habitat degradation, pollution, and human disturbances. These areas are meticulously chosen and managed to support diverse bird species, encompassing forests, wetlands, grasslands, and coastal regions. By preserving extensive, contiguous habitats, they mitigate the risks of habitat fragmentation, a significant threat that isolates bird populations, diminishes genetic diversity, and heightens susceptibility to environmental changes and stochastic events. Within protected areas, birds encounter stable conditions vital for feeding, breeding, and sheltering, thereby bolstering their survival prospects amidst escalating environmental pressures.

India's protected areas harbor an impressive array of birdlife, encompassing numerous endemic and endangered species. Keoladeo National Park in Rajasthan, a UNESCO World Heritage site, hosts a plethora of migratory birds like the Siberian crane, bar-headed goose, and painted stork during the winter months. Similarly, Sundarbans National Park in West Bengal, with its extensive mangrove forests, serves as critical habitat for species such as the brown-winged kingfisher and masked finfoot. These protected zones play an indispensable role in conserving avian biodiversity by safeguarding habitats vital for diverse bird populations.

Habitat corridors, also known as ecological or wildlife corridors, constitute another crucial facet of avian conservation amidst climate change. These corridors, which link protected areas, enable birds to navigate diverse landscapes, access essential resources, and traverse breeding grounds. Vital for maintaining genetic diversity and facilitating seasonal migrations, these corridors assume heightened significance as climate change alters habitat distribution. In regions like the Western Ghats and Eastern Himalayas, networks of habitat corridors connect protected areas, enabling species such as the Malabar trogon and rufous-necked hornbill to adapt to varying elevations and microclimates, ensuring their survival amid shifting environmental dynamics.

However, establishing and preserving habitat corridors entail overcoming ecological and anthropogenic hurdles. Land-use changes, including deforestation, agriculture, and urbanization, often disrupt or obliterate natural corridors. Effective corridor design hinges on understanding species-specific needs and behaviors, such as their preferred habitats and movement patterns. Collaboration with local communities and stakeholders is crucial to promote land-use practices compatible with conservation goals, ensuring the integrity and efficacy of these vital ecological connections.

Efforts to restore degraded or fragmented habitat corridors involve initiatives such as native species reforestation, wetland rehabilitation, and invasive species removal. These restoration endeavors not only enhance connectivity but also bolster landscape health and resilience, benefiting a broad spectrum of wildlife alongside avian populations. Community engagement through education, awareness campaigns, and sustainable livelihood projects fosters local stewardship, fortifying long-term commitment to avian habitat conservation.

5.2 Research and Monitoring: Understanding Impacts and Developing Mitigation Strategies

In India, understanding the impact of climate change on bird populations and devising effective mitigation strategies requires rigorous research and monitoring. Climate change presents myriad challenges to avian species, including altered temperature regimes, shifting precipitation patterns, intensified extreme weather events, and habitat degradation. Systematic research and comprehensive monitoring are indispensable for acquiring the data needed to comprehend these transformations, anticipate future consequences, and guide conservation initiatives aimed at safeguarding bird populations. Central to addressing climate impacts on birds is the establishment of robust research frameworks capable of meticulously measuring and analyzing changes in bird populations and their habitats. Long-term studies are particularly valuable for revealing trends that short-term investigations may overlook. Such studies can uncover shifts in species distributions, changes in breeding and migration timings, and fluctuations in population sizes, critical for understanding bird responses to climate change and identifying vulnerable species.

DATA SHEET - VI
IMPACT OF POACHING AND ILLEGAL TRADE ON AVIAN SPECIES IN INDIA

Study Title	Key Findings	Citation
A star attraction: The illegal trade in Indian Star Tortoises	The study documents the illegal trade of 55,000 individuals poached from one trade hub in India. Domestic demand persists.	[82]
Trends in CITES listed bird's trade in South Asian countries in view of evolution of Indian laws during last four decades	Discusses the illegal trade of wildlife, emphasizing changes in Indian laws affecting wildlife trade.	[83]
Poaching, Illegal Wildlife Trade, and Bushmeat	Highlights the extent of illegal wildlife trade and poaching in	[84]

Hunting in India and South Asia	India, covering numerous species including birds.	
An Analysis of Criminal Laws against Poaching Animals and Wildlife Trafficking	Discusses the historical and current legal framework in India aimed at curbing poaching and illegal wildlife trade.	[85]
Illegal avian and reptilian pets: Global perspectives and challenges	Addresses the challenges of illegal trade in avian species, including African Grey Parrots and Indian Star Tortoises.	[86]
A Study on Wildlife Trafficking and the Issue of Poaching: The Law and Judicial Outlook	Examines wildlife trafficking and poaching, focusing on the legal and judicial outlook in India.	[87]
Market for Animal Body Parts and Tiger Poaching: National Environmental Laws to Counter This Scenery	Discusses illegal wildlife trade markets and efforts to counteract poaching in India.	[88]
Illegal wildlife trade is threatening conservation in the transboundary landscape of Western Himalaya	Focuses on illegal wildlife trade in the Kailash Sacred Landscape, affecting conservation efforts.	[89]
Current wildlife crime (Indian scenario): major challenges and prevention approaches	Highlights the major hubs for wildlife trafficking in India and the ongoing challenges.	[90]
Trends and patterns of illegal wildlife hunting and trading in Uttar Pradesh, India	Examines illegal wildlife hunting and trading, highlighting key species affected.	[91]
Insights from the media into the bird trade in India: an analysis of reported seizures	Analyzes media reports on bird trade seizures in India to understand the scale of the issue.	[91]
Poaching and Illegal Trade of Wildlife: What Do the Media Say for the Nepali-Chinese and Nepali-Indian Border?	Discusses poaching and wildlife trade at the Nepali-Indian border, affecting multiple species including birds.	[92]

A Critical Analysis on the Impact of Poaching of Animals on Environment and the Laws Prohibiting It in India	Examines the environmental impact of poaching and the effectiveness of prohibitive laws in India.	[93]
Do wildlife crimes against less charismatic species go unnoticed? A case study of Golden Jackal Canis aureus Linnaeus, 1758 poaching and trade in India	Investigates the lesser-known impacts of wildlife crimes on species like the Golden Jackal in India.	[94]
Poaching, habitat loss and the decline of neotropical parrots: A comparative spatial analysis	Compares the impact of poaching and habitat loss on neotropical parrots, with relevance to Indian avian species.	[95]
Poaching and illegal wildlife trade in western Argentina	Highlights the illegal trade of birds used as pets and its impact on biodiversity.	[96]
Trade bans: a perfect storm for poaching?	Discusses the unintended consequences of trade bans on the rates of poaching and illegal wildlife trade.	[97]
Illegal wildlife trade in India	Provides an overview of the illegal wildlife trade in India and its implications for conservation.	[98]
Sustainable development, poaching, and illegal wildlife trade in India	Reviews wildlife policy development and the impact of poaching on bird species in India.	[99]
The illegal wildlife trade: Inside the world of poachers, smugglers and traders	Explores the world of illegal wildlife trade, including bird poaching and trafficking.	[100]

CHAPTER 6

Poaching and Illegal Trade: The Wilful Damage

1. Defying Legal Protections: The Persistence of Poaching

1.1 Targeted Species: Endangered Birds and Lucrative Markets

The illegal poaching and trade of birds in India pose a significant threat to biodiversity, particularly affecting endangered species highly coveted in lucrative markets. Despite stringent legal protections both nationally and internationally, poaching persists, driven by diverse demands such as the pet trade, traditional medicine, and status symbols. Effective conservation strategies necessitate a deep understanding of targeted species and the dynamics of their exploitation. India boasts a unique avian diversity, yet this richness faces escalating peril from poaching targeting already vulnerable species amid habitat loss and environmental shifts. Critically endangered birds like the Indian bustard, red-headed vulture, and black-breasted parrotbill endure heightened threats from illegal hunting and trade. These species, valued for their rarity and profitability in domestic and global markets, confront perilous declines.

The Indian bustard, critically endangered with a population of fewer than 150 individuals, remains a prime poaching target prized for its meat and feathers. Habitat encroachment exacerbates vulnerability, despite protection under the Wildlife Protection Act of 1972, complicating enforcement due to vast, remote habitats. Persistent demand for bustard feathers in rituals and its meat as a delicacy propels ongoing illegal hunting, dangerously pushing the species towards extinction. Similarly imperiled, the red-headed vulture faces targeted poaching for its body parts, valued in traditional medicines. The species suffers from population declines linked to factors like habitat loss, poisoning from veterinary drugs, and cultural practices. Despite legal safeguards, the demand endures, imperiling both the vulture's survival and its ecological role in disease control and scavenging.

Parrots and parakeets, including the black-breasted parrotbill and Alexandrine parakeet, face rampant capture for the illegal pet trade, prized for their vivid plumage and mimicry. Their extraction from the wild for global markets inflicts high mortality rates due to stress and harsh conditions during transport. Weak enforcement against poaching, hindered by corruption and limited resources, empowers traffickers to operate with impunity, further jeopardizing wild populations.

1.2 Methods and Motivations: Feathers, Eggs, and the Live Bird Trade

Poaching and the illicit trade of birds persist as grave threats to avian populations in India, despite stringent legal safeguards. Motivations for these activities are diverse, driven by economic, cultural, and social factors, each tailored to meet specific market demands. Feathers, eggs, and live birds are coveted commodities, valued for their aesthetic appeal, symbolic significance, and economic profitability. Feathers, particularly from species like peacocks and hornbills, are prized for their vibrant hues and cultural symbolism, often used in traditional costumes and religious ceremonies. The clandestine nature of feather collection involves trapping, hunting, or scavenging from nests, challenging law enforcement efforts due to concealable transport methods and high demand. Egg poaching poses another critical threat, driven by both commercial gain and personal interest. Eggs of endangered species like the great Indian bustard are targeted despite protective measures, disrupting breeding success and conservation efforts. Poachers locate nests through surveys or by tracking adult birds, extracting eggs with methods that disturb nesting sites and reduce reproductive outcomes. Meanwhile, the live bird trade, primarily for the pet industry, is pervasive and devastating. Species such as parakeets and owls are captured using traps, nets, and decoys, often resulting in high mortality rates during capture and transport. These practices not only harm individual birds but also disrupt ecosystem functions and biodiversity.

2. A Multi-Billion Dollar Crime: The Illegal Wildlife Trade

2.1 Global Reach and Transnational Networks: A Lucrative Black Market

The illegal wildlife trade represents a sprawling industry of global proportions, driven by immense demand and substantial profits. Operating across borders, this illicit market encompasses intricate transnational networks that facilitate the poaching, trafficking, and sale of wildlife and their parts. Among the most vulnerable are birds, imperiling their populations and disrupting ecosystems on a significant scale. The global reach and sophistication of these networks present formidable challenges for conservationists and law enforcement agencies worldwide. Birds hold a coveted position within the illegal wildlife trade for their vibrant plumage, melodious songs, and exotic allure, making them sought-after commodities as pets, decorative items, and symbols of prestige. This trade encompasses live birds, feathers, eggs, and various body parts, catering to diverse segments of the black market. The demand originates from regions spanning Asia, the Middle East, Europe, and the Americas, where exotic birds are prized for private collections, zoos, and breeding programs, driving poaching activities particularly in biodiversity-rich areas such as India, home to many unique and endangered species.

India stands as a notable source country for trafficked birds, with species like the Indian peafowl, Alexandrine parakeet, and black-headed munia frequently targeted. Poachers employ an array of methods from simple traps and nets to sophisticated techniques involving decoys and sound lures, operating in remote, inaccessible regions that challenge law enforcement efforts. Once captured, birds endure perilous transportation routes, often resulting in high mortality rates, underscoring the harsh realities of the illicit trade. The illegal bird trade thrives on well-organized transnational networks characterized by meticulous coordination and secrecy, involving a spectrum of participants from local poachers and middlemen to transporters and international buyers. Beginning with local hunters driven by economic incentives, birds move through a chain that consolidates and transports them to urban centers or border areas for onward distribution.

Transportation poses a critical phase, necessitating intricate logistics to avoid detection. Birds are concealed within vehicle compartments, hidden among legal goods, or carried by couriers with falsified documents. Corruption and lax enforcement at key entry and exit points facilitate the trafficking process, exploiting legal loopholes and bribing officials to ease the movement of illicit cargo. Upon reaching destination countries, birds enter various sectors of the black market, sold in pet shops, markets, or online platforms. Rare and exotic species command exorbitant prices, with buyers willing to pay substantial sums for prized specimens. Feathers and other body parts satisfy demand for ornamental, medicinal, or cultural purposes, further fueling the market's segments.

Addressing the global scourge of the illegal bird trade demands a concerted international response, involving strengthened legal frameworks, enhanced enforcement capabilities, and robust international cooperation. Instruments such as the Convention on International Trade in Endangered Species of Wild Fauna and Flora (CITES) provide a foundational framework for regulating the trade in endangered species, though their effectiveness hinges on rigorous implementation and enforcement at the national level. Law enforcement agencies confront multifaceted challenges in combating the illegal bird trade, compounded by its covert nature that frustrates detection and investigation efforts. Poachers and traffickers continually adapt tactics to evade capture, exploiting new routes and techniques while enforcement agencies, often under-resourced and understaffed, struggle with limited tools and training to effectively combat wildlife crime.

2.2 Threats to Native and Exotic Species: Unsustainable Practices and Population Decline

The illegal wildlife trade in India represents a formidable threat to both native and exotic bird species, with profound implications for biodiversity conservation. Driven by lucrative profits and persistent demand, this illicit industry encompasses poaching, trafficking, and illegal sales, precipitating severe population declines that jeopardize species survival. India's diverse avian fauna, harboring numerous endemic species such as the critically endangered great Indian bustard, Bengal florican, and Jerdon's courser, confronts imminent peril from these unsustainable practices. These birds, valued for their unique traits like vibrant plumage and distinctive calls, are targeted despite legal protections, exacerbating their dwindling numbers and compromising their reproductive viability.

Exotic bird species, trafficked through India en route to international markets, also endure harsh consequences of the illegal trade. Parrots, macaws, and cockatoos from regions like South America and Southeast Asia suffer high mortality rates due to brutal handling during capture and transport. Packed into cramped containers without adequate food or water, these birds endure extreme stress on lengthy journeys, amplifying their plight. Moreover, the trade's impact extends beyond direct exploitation to encompass habitat destruction, disrupting ecological balance and imperiling entire ecosystems dependent on avian roles as pollinators, seed dispersers, and pest controllers.

The historical and cultural significance of bird feathers fuels continued poaching, as species like the Indian peafowl and paradise flycatcher are coveted for traditional attire and decorative items. This demand intensifies during breeding seasons, heightening vulnerability and impeding population recovery. Similarly, the collection of bird eggs for consumption disrupts reproductive cycles and nesting habitats, further compromising species survival. The illicit trade's toll extends to live bird trafficking for the pet industry, where captured birds endure trauma, disease, and often premature death, while introducing exotic species risks destabilizing local ecosystems and native species dynamics.

Socio-economic factors underpinning the illegal bird trade are intricate, influenced by poverty, limited opportunities, and economic incentives in rural communities. For many, poaching and trading birds represent a vital income stream, perpetuating a cycle where diminished populations escalate market demand and prices. This economic dependency sustains illicit activities despite regulatory measures, posing enduring challenges to conservation efforts and biodiversity protection.

3. The Human Cost of Poaching and Illegal Trade

3.1 Zoonotic Diseases and Public Health Risks: Disease Transmission from Birds to Humans

The convergence of poaching, illegal trade, and public health presents a multifaceted challenge, particularly concerning zoonotic diseases transmitted from birds to humans. In India, as elsewhere, cultural practices, food habits, and economic activities drive human-wildlife interaction, amplifying disease transmission risks. Birds, acting as reservoirs and vectors of pathogens, pose substantial public health threats when populations are disrupted by poaching and illegal trade. Understanding these dynamics necessitates examining specific diseases, transmission pathways, and their broader implications for human health and conservation efforts. Avian influenza, or bird flu, stands as a prominent zoonotic concern associated with both wild and domestic birds. The virus, capable of infecting various bird species including waterfowl and poultry, spreads rapidly aided by migratory patterns and interactions between wild and domestic birds. While most avian influenza strains do not directly infect humans, certain subtypes like H5N1 and H7N9 have sporadically caused severe outbreaks with high mortality rates. The illegal trade in live birds, involving mixing species from diverse habitats, heightens the risk of virus transmission and mutation, potentially leading to new strains capable of human-to-human transmission.

Salmonellosis, caused by Salmonella bacteria, represents another zoonotic disease associated with birds. Birds can carry Salmonella asymptomatically or show mild symptoms, shedding bacteria through feces, saliva, and feathers. Humans typically contract Salmonella through direct contact with contaminated birds or their environments, such as aviaries and markets. Symptoms include gastrointestinal distress such as diarrhea and fever. The unsanitary conditions prevalent in illegal bird trade-overcrowded and unhygienic during transportation and captivity-elevate the risk of bacterial transmission and subsequent human outbreaks. Psittacosis, also known as parrot fever, stems from Chlamydia psittaci bacteria found in parrots and related birds. Infected birds shed the bacterium through feces and respiratory secretions, which can aerosolize and be inhaled by humans. In humans, psittacosis ranges from mild flu-like symptoms to severe pneumonia, potentially fatal if untreated. The illegal trade in exotic parrots and similar birds exacerbates psittacosis transmission, transporting infected birds across borders and exposing handlers to the bacterium. Poor hygiene and inadequate veterinary care during transport intensify disease risks.

3.2 Livelihood Loss and Community Impacts: Disruption of Sustainable Hunting Practices

The illegal poaching and trade of birds have profound repercussions that extend well beyond ecological impacts. Among these consequences is the disruption of longstanding sustainable hunting practices, which are deeply intertwined with the livelihoods and cultural traditions of many indigenous and rural communities, particularly in India. These practices, rooted in a profound knowledge of local ecosystems and guided by customary laws, have historically balanced human needs with wildlife conservation efforts. However, the rise of poaching and illegal trade has severely compromised these practices, leading to detrimental effects across social, economic, and cultural dimensions.

Central to the issue is the direct loss of livelihood for communities reliant on sustainable hunting. In many rural areas, hunting birds not only provides food but also generates income through the sale of meat, feathers, and other parts. The illicit demand for exotic pets, traditional medicine ingredients, and other uses has resulted in the overexploitation of bird populations, making it increasingly difficult for hunters to sustain their livelihoods. Consequently, families face economic instability, forcing them to seek less reliable sources of income, thereby exacerbating poverty within the community. Beyond economic repercussions, the disruption of sustainable hunting practices undermines the social and cultural fabric of these communities. Hunting traditionally serves as a communal activity that fosters social bonds and preserves cultural identities through rituals and shared knowledge of nature. Yet, as poaching renders traditional hunting unsustainable, these cultural practices erode, potentially disconnecting younger generations from their heritage and weakening community cohesion.

Ecologically, the consequences are equally dire. Sustainable hunting practices typically maintain ecosystem balance by selectively managing wildlife populations. In contrast, poaching targets rare and endangered species indiscriminately, upsetting ecological equilibrium. This imbalance can disrupt critical ecosystem services such as seed dispersal and pest control, which in turn affects agricultural productivity and exacerbates economic hardship for communities reliant on these natural resources.

4. Combating the Illegal Trade: Law Enforcement and Conservation Efforts

4.1 Strengthening Enforcement Mechanisms: Addressing Corruption and Improving Patrols

The illegal bird trade in India presents a formidable threat to biodiversity, disrupting ecosystems and precipitating the decline of numerous species. Strengthening enforcement measures is paramount, necessitating a concerted effort to combat corruption and bolster patrolling initiatives. Addressing this multifaceted issue requires a nuanced understanding of existing enforcement dynamics, the pervasive impact of corruption, and strategies to enhance the efficacy of patrols. Enforcement mechanisms in India have long grappled with systemic challenges, chief among them being corruption within wildlife protection agencies. This pervasive issue undermines enforcement efforts significantly. When officials succumb to bribery or compromise, poachers and traders exploit loopholes, evading detection and prosecution with impunity. Corruption manifests at various levels, from frontline rangers accepting bribes to higher-ranking officials turning a blind eye to illicit activities, creating a porous enforcement landscape where laws are inconsistently upheld.

Combatting corruption demands a comprehensive approach, integrating preventive and punitive measures. Preventively, robust training programs for wildlife enforcement personnel are crucial, emphasizing ethical standards and the enduring benefits of wildlife conservation. Regular refresher courses are essential to sustain high ethical norms and update officers on cutting-edge conservation techniques and technologies. Transparency in operational protocols and a structured system for reporting corruption allegations are imperative, reinforced by safeguards for whistleblowers to deter reprisals. Establishing an independent oversight body to investigate corruption allegations and enforce disciplinary actions can further fortify integrity within enforcement agencies.

On the punitive front, enforcing stringent penalties against corrupt officials is indispensable, ensuring swift dismissal and legal recourse where warranted. Publicizing cases of accountability serves as a deterrent, bolstered by collaborations with anti-corruption bodies to enhance investigative capacities.

5. A Sustainable Future: Balancing Conservation and Livelihoods

5.1 Empowering Local Communities: Creating Alternative Income Sources and Fostering Stewardship

Empowering local communities is pivotal for cultivating a sustainable future that harmonizes conservation with livelihood needs, particularly in regions like India where communities coexist closely with forests and wildlife. The challenge lies in bolstering economic support for these communities while instilling a sense of stewardship towards their natural environment. This dual approach not only safeguards biodiversity but also enhances the welfare of people reliant on natural resources for their sustenance. One effective strategy involves establishing alternative income streams that do not rely on activities detrimental to wildlife, such as poaching and illicit trade. Ecotourism emerges as a promising avenue in this regard, offering communities financial benefits derived from their natural landscapes and biodiversity. Initiatives like bird-watching tours, guided nature walks, and wildlife photography expeditions can generate income, provided they are meticulously planned with investments in infrastructure and local guide training. Engaging community members in the management of ecotourism ventures not only creates employment opportunities but also fosters a vested interest in environmental conservation.

Promoting local crafts and artisanal goods represents another viable pathway towards sustainable livelihoods. Many indigenous communities possess unique skills in traditional crafts like weaving, pottery, and carving. By facilitating market access and promoting cooperative efforts among artisans, communities can develop sustainable income sources. Integrating conservation principles into product branding enhances market appeal and underscores the community's dedication to preserving their natural heritage. Additionally, agroforestry and sustainable agricultural practices offer opportunities to diversify livelihoods while supporting conservation goals. Agroforestry integrates trees and shrubs into agricultural landscapes, enriching biodiversity and providing supplementary income through the sale of fruits, nuts, and timber. Training in sustainable farming techniques such as organic farming and water conservation not only boosts productivity but also reduces reliance on forest resources, bolstering food security and economic stability for farming communities.

5.2 Promoting Sustainable Hunting Practices: Ensuring Long-Term Conservation Strategies

Empowering local communities is pivotal for cultivating a sustainable future that harmonizes conservation with livelihood needs, particularly in regions like India where communities coexist closely with forests and wildlife. The challenge lies in bolstering economic support for these communities while instilling a sense of stewardship towards their natural environment. This dual approach not only safeguards biodiversity but also enhances the welfare of people reliant on natural resources for their sustenance. One effective strategy involves establishing alternative income streams that do not rely on activities detrimental to wildlife, such as poaching and illicit trade. Ecotourism emerges as a promising avenue in this regard, offering communities financial benefits derived from their natural landscapes and biodiversity. Initiatives like bird-watching tours, guided nature walks, and wildlife photography expeditions can generate income, provided they are meticulously planned with investments in infrastructure and local guide training. Engaging community members in the management of ecotourism ventures not only creates employment opportunities but also fosters a vested interest in environmental conservation.

Promoting local crafts and artisanal goods represents another viable pathway towards sustainable livelihoods. Many indigenous communities possess unique skills in traditional crafts like weaving, pottery, and carving. By facilitating market access and promoting cooperative efforts among artisans, communities can develop sustainable income sources. Integrating conservation principles into product branding enhances market appeal and underscores the community's dedication to preserving their natural heritage. Additionally, agroforestry and sustainable agricultural practices offer opportunities to diversify livelihoods while supporting conservation goals. Agroforestry integrates trees and shrubs into agricultural landscapes, enriching biodiversity and providing supplementary income through the sale of fruits, nuts, and timber. Training in sustainable farming techniques such as organic farming and water conservation not only boosts productivity but also reduces reliance on forest resources, bolstering food security and economic stability for farming communities.

Community-based conservation programs further empower local populations by involving them directly in the management and protection of natural resources. Activities such as patrolling protected areas, monitoring wildlife, and participating in habitat restoration initiatives instill a sense of ownership and responsibility among community members.

DATA SHEET - VII
IMPACT OF INFRASTRUCTURE DEVELOPMENT ON AVIAN SPECIES IN INDIA

Study Title	Key Findings	Citation
Framing ecologically sound policy on linear intrusions affecting wildlife habitats	Risk of disease spread and bird collisions with infrastructure such as cranes.	[101]
A case study on seasonal variation in roadkill mortality on National Highway 715	High mortality rates of birds due to vehicular collisions in Assam, India.	[102]
Impact of chaotic urbanisation on Bengaluru's urban avian diversity	Increased risk of bird ailments and deaths due to collisions with urban structures.	[62]
Edge effect of busy high traffic roads on the nest site selection of birds inside the city area: Guild response	High mortality of birds due to traffic collisions in Udaipur, Rajasthan, India.	[103]
Wildlife-vehicle collisions in Lanzarote biosphere reserve, Canary Islands	High collision rates and mortality of birds due to vehicular traffic.	[104]

Integrating large mammal behaviour and traffic flow to determine traversability of roads with heterogeneous traffic on a Central Indian Highway	High risk of wildlife-vehicle collisions affecting birds and mammals in Central India.	[105]
Responses of birds and mammals to long-established wind farms in India	Significant mortality of birds due to collision with wind turbines.	[106]
Predicting pedestrian crash locations in urban India	High collision rates involving birds in urban areas due to infrastructure development.	[106]
Wildlife mortality on National Highway 72 and 74 across the Rajaji National Park	High incidence of bird mortality due to vehicular collisions in North India.	[107]
Roads, sensitive habitats and wildlife: environmental guideline for India and South Asia	Significant bird mortality due to collisions with infrastructure in Punjab, India.	[108]
The ecological effects of linear infrastructure and traffic: challenges and opportunities of rapid global growth	Increased bird mortality due to collisions with linear infrastructures such as roads and power lines.	[109]
Reducing collisions with structures	Analysis of bird collisions with various structures, including recommendations for mitigation.	[110]
Mortality in wildlife due to transportation	Extensive bird mortality due to collisions with vehicles.	[111]
Bird collisions with glass: an annotated bibliography	Extensive data on bird collisions with glass structures and mitigation strategies.	[112]
Estimates of Avian Mortality Attributed to Vehicle Collisions in Canada	Significant avian mortality rates due to vehicle collisions, applicable to India.	[113]
Birds crossing over roads: species, flight heights and infrastructure use	Analysis of bird species at risk of collision with vehicles, with implications for urban planning.	[114]

CHAPTER 7

Collisions with Infrastructure: Urban Development Hazards

1. A Modern Threat: Birds and Man-Made Structures

1.1 Power Lines and Communication Towers: Silent Killers During Migration

Power lines and communication towers present a pervasive threat to avian species, particularly during migration, constituting a significant concern for conservation efforts globally, including in India. Migration represents a critical period in the life cycle of many bird species, involving extensive journeys across varied landscapes and habitats. Birds rely on innate navigational abilities and environmental cues during migration, yet the proliferation of man-made structures poses substantial risks. Power lines, ubiquitous in urban and rural areas, intersect crucial migratory routes and present collision hazards, especially in low light or adverse weather conditions. Larger birds like raptors and cranes are particularly vulnerable to collisions due to their size and flight behaviors, often resulting in fatal injuries.

The expansion of power grids to meet growing energy demands further exacerbates the issue, fragmenting habitats and intensifying risks for migrating birds. Wetlands, forests, and other vital habitats face increased disturbance from power line installations, impacting species reliant on these areas during migration. Similarly, communication towers, towering structures equipped with guy wires, pose significant threats to birds navigating migratory flyways. These towers, often adorned with steady-burning lights for aircraft visibility, attract and disorient birds, increasing collision risks, a phenomenon known as "tower kill."

1.2 Wind Turbines and Solar Panels: Emerging Threats and Mitigation Strategies

Wind turbines and solar panels have become integral components of contemporary renewable energy systems, marking pivotal strides towards sustainable energy generation. However, these installations also pose emergent perils to avian populations, particularly in biodiverse regions like India. Addressing these challenges and devising effective mitigation strategies is imperative to harmonize the pursuit of renewable energy with avian conservation. Wind turbines, characterized by their towering stature and rotating blades, present substantial collision risks to birds. Typically sited in expansive, wind-rich locales-often coinciding with prime bird habitats and migratory paths-these structures pose a lethal threat, especially to soaring birds like raptors and large migratory species. The swift rotation of turbine blades, particularly at high speeds, poses challenges for birds to detect and evade, resulting in fatal collisions. Studies underscore significant bird mortalities at wind farms, with some sites reporting hundreds of fatalities annually.

Strategic placement of wind turbines in crucial habitats and migration corridors exacerbates these hazards. Many wind farms occupy coastal zones, ridgelines, and open plains-preferred by birds for feeding, nesting, and transit. Migration seasons heighten collision risks, as exhausted birds navigating long distances may struggle to maneuver around turbines. Nocturnal migrants, reliant on celestial cues for navigation, face disorientation from turbine presence, further elevating collision risks. Mitigating these impacts entails technological innovations and meticulous site selection. Innovations include bird-sensitive turbine designs and detection systems employing radar or cameras to halt operations temporarily upon bird detection. Acoustic and visual deterrents, such as lights and sounds, aim to alert birds and redirect their flight paths away from turbines. Site assessments before wind farm construction are crucial, identifying high avian activity areas to avoid potential collision hotspots. Adaptive management practices, like adjusting turbine operations during peak migration, offer additional safeguards.

2. Urban Environments: A Labyrinth of Risks

2.1 Buildings with Reflective Glass: Disorientation and Collisions

Reflective glass buildings pose a significant threat to birds in urban environments, often overlooked amidst modern architectural landscapes. These structures, characterized by mirrored surfaces, contribute substantially to bird disorientation and collisions. Birds, unable to distinguish glass as a barrier, frequently collide with these surfaces, resulting in injury and mortality. This issue is particularly acute in densely populated urban areas where such buildings form intricate, hazardous mazes for both resident and migrating bird populations. The challenge posed by reflective glass lies in its ability to mirror the surrounding environment, creating illusions of continuous habitat. During daylight hours, reflections of trees and open skies deceive birds into mistaking these surfaces for real spaces. At night, artificial lights within buildings further attract birds, compounding the risk of collisions, especially during migration seasons when urban areas see increased avian traffic.

The consequences of bird collisions with reflective glass extend beyond individual fatalities to broader ecological impacts. Many affected species already contend with declining populations due to habitat loss, climate change, and other human activities. Each collision represents a loss to overall populations, particularly detrimental for species with limited numbers or declining trends. Moreover, the loss of breeding adults directly impacts reproductive success and population stability. Addressing this threat requires a comprehensive approach integrating architectural design, urban planning, and public awareness. A key strategy involves employing bird-safe glass in building design, utilizing patterns that birds can perceive to avoid collisions. Techniques such as etching, fritting, or applying UV coatings visible to birds but not humans have proven effective. Even simple patterns like stripes or dots, when sufficiently spaced, significantly reduce collision rates.

Architectural solutions also include minimizing reflective glass use and incorporating non-reflective or opaque materials. Additional measures like window screens, shutters, and external shades help mitigate reflections and physically deter birds from striking glass surfaces. These modifications can be applied to new constructions or retrofitted onto existing buildings to enhance bird safety. Urban planning plays a crucial role by strategically siting bird-friendly buildings along migration routes and areas of high avian activity. Protecting and enhancing green spaces within urban landscapes provides alternative, collision-free habitats for birds. Bird-friendly urban districts, adhering to safe design principles, further promote avian conservation efforts within city environments.

2.2 Traffic-Related Stressors: Impacting Bird Populations in Cities

Urban environments, with their intricate web of roads and bustling vehicular activity, impose a myriad of challenges on bird populations. The rapid urbanization sweeping through India has intensified stressors linked to traffic, profoundly affecting the well-being, behavior, and survival of city-dwelling birds. These stressors encompass collisions with vehicles, noise pollution, air pollution, habitat fragmentation, and alterations in food availability and quality. Understanding these impacts and devising effective mitigation strategies are pivotal to safeguarding urban bird populations. Among the most conspicuous consequences of urban traffic on birds are collisions with vehicles. Birds navigating low over roads or crossing busy thoroughfares face perilous encounters with cars, trucks, and other vehicles, often resulting in severe injury or mortality. Such collisions exert disproportionate pressure on vulnerable species with limited reproductive capacity, particularly juvenile birds and inexperienced flyers ill-equipped to navigate the hazards of urban landscapes safely. In addition to physical collisions, the ceaseless clamor of traffic poses a pervasive and detrimental stressor. The din of engines, horns, and urban commotion disrupts vital avian communications essential for mating rituals, territorial defense, and parent-offspring interactions. Many bird species rely on vocalizations to attract mates and establish territories, yet these signals often drown in the cacophony of urban noise. Some birds compensate by amplifying their calls, a costly effort that may not suffice amidst the din. Air pollution emerges as another critical issue stemming from vehicular emissions, including particulates, nitrogen oxides, and volatile compounds. These pollutants degrade air quality, compromising bird health with respiratory ailments, weakened immune systems, and heightened susceptibility to diseases. Furthermore, polluted air adversely affects insect populations, a crucial dietary staple for many bird species, thus further undermining avian well-being through bioaccumulation of contaminants.

The construction of roads and urban infrastructure exacerbates the problem through habitat fragmentation, isolating green spaces into patches insufficient to sustain robust bird populations. Fragmented habitats curtail bird mobility, limiting access to essential resources like nesting sites and food, and increasing vulnerability to environmental shifts and diseases. Species dependent on expansive, contiguous habitats, such as migratory birds and raptors, face heightened risk from habitat fragmentation. Moreover, urbanization alters food dynamics, reshaping the distribution and quality of natural food sources like insects, seeds, and fruits. Roads may obstruct access to feeding areas or contaminate nearby food sources with vehicle emissions, undermining the nutritional health of urban birds. Additionally, reliance on human-provided food sources alters natural foraging behaviors, further compromising avian fitness.

3. Case Studies: Avian Casualties and the Need for Solutions

Urban environments present formidable challenges to bird populations, resulting in significant avian casualties from multiple sources such as reflective glass buildings, vehicular traffic, communication towers, power lines, and light pollution. Understanding the breadth of these challenges requires delving into specific urban case studies that underscore the struggles birds face and the innovative strategies deployed to mitigate these threats. In Mumbai, a hub of rapid urbanization and high-density glass structures, migratory birds often collide with reflective surfaces, exacerbated by the city's position along major migration routes. The Bombay Natural History Society (BNHS) has documented substantial bird fatalities, particularly affecting species like the Asian koel and common myna. To combat this, BNHS advocates for bird-friendly glass and educates the public on collision prevention.

Delhi grapples with high bird mortality rates around communication towers, where nocturnal migrants like the Indian pitta are disoriented by bright lights. Collaborative efforts by the Wildlife Institute of India (WII) and telecom companies have introduced bird-friendly lighting and deflectors, reducing fatalities notably. In Chennai, extensive road networks pose dangers to species like the Black kite due to frequent bird-vehicle collisions. The Madras Naturalists' Society initiates green corridors with native vegetation and wildlife crossings to safeguard urban biodiversity.

Bangalore addresses light pollution affecting nocturnal species such as the Indian nightjar, with the Nature Conservation Foundation (NCF) promoting downward-facing and motion-activated lighting to preserve natural behaviors. Hyderabad mitigates power line hazards with bird diverters and insulation, supported by local groups like Hyderabad Birding Pals, reducing electrocution incidents among species like the Painted stork.

Kolkata's habitat loss through urban development affects wetland-dependent species like the Purple heron, countered by Wetlands International South Asia's advocacy for protected areas and habitat restoration. Ahmedabad tackles reflective glass and light pollution issues with bird-friendly designs and community education led by the Gujarat Ecological Education and Research (GEER) Foundation.

Pune grapples with infrastructure expansion impacting bird habitats, addressed by the Ela Foundation through research, advocacy for bird-friendly building codes, and habitat restoration projects. Goa confronts habitat loss from tourism infrastructure, combated by the Goa Bird Conservation Network (GBCN) through sustainable planning and awareness campaigns.

3.1 The Tragic Fate of Migratory Ospreys: Collision with Wind Turbines

The plight of migratory ospreys colliding with wind turbines illustrates the unintended consequences of modern infrastructure on wildlife. Ospreys, renowned for their majestic wingspans and adept hunting skills, embark on arduous migrations spanning thousands of kilometers from breeding grounds in northern climes to wintering havens in warmer regions. Yet, this remarkable journey has become perilous amid the expanding footprint of wind energy projects. Wind turbines, touted as eco-friendly alternatives to fossil fuels, pose significant hazards to birds, particularly visually reliant species like ospreys. With blades exceeding 100 meters in diameter and swift rotations, turbines present formidable aerial obstacles. Ospreys, often flying at altitudes intersecting with turbine heights, face heightened risks of collisions during their medium-altitude foraging flights and migration along coastlines, rivers, and lakes-prime locations for wind farms due to consistent wind patterns.

Compounding the issue is ospreys' sharp focus on aquatic prey, making them less attentive to airborne impediments like turbine blades, which can blur visually, especially under certain lighting conditions. Collisions not only threaten individual ospreys but also imperil population dynamics; these birds reproduce slowly, typically rearing only one to three chicks annually per pair, and fatalities among mature breeders can disrupt long-term viability. Efforts to mitigate these impacts include strategic turbine siting away from migration routes and critical osprey habitats, informed by comprehensive environmental assessments. Technological innovations such as contrasting blade painting and ultraviolet patterns enhance turbine visibility to avian species, potentially curbing collisions. Advanced radar systems offer real-time bird detection capabilities, automatically halting turbine operations to safeguard vulnerable flocks, albeit at considerable technological and financial investment.

4. Finding Solutions: Bird-Friendly Infrastructure Design

4.1 Marking Power Lines and Using Bird Diverters: Reducing Collision Risks

Bird collisions with power lines pose a significant threat to avian species globally, with particular intensity observed in India amidst rapid urbanization. Across varied habitats like wetlands, forests, and open fields, proliferating power lines amplify risks to birds, especially during migration and daily foraging. These collisions often prove fatal, exacerbating declines in vulnerable species populations. Mitigating these risks through bird-friendly infrastructure, including marking power lines and using bird diverters, has emerged as an effective strategy.

Power lines pose inherent dangers to birds for several reasons. Their thin profile and background blending make them hard to detect, especially in adverse conditions like fog or twilight. Birds, particularly large species with limited maneuverability such as cranes and raptors, are especially vulnerable due to their flight paths intersecting with these lines. Marking power lines is a straightforward yet powerful method to reduce collisions. Various markers, from colored balls to reflective tapes, enhance visibility depending on environmental factors and bird species present. Studies show brightly colored markers can decrease collisions by up to 60%, while reflective materials provide continuous visibility day and night.

Bird diverters offer another innovative solution. These devices, like the FireFly with reflective and glowing elements, create dynamic visual cues that alert birds to the presence of power lines. Implementations have shown diverters can reduce collisions by 80%, underscoring their effectiveness in safeguarding avian populations. Strategic deployment of these measures requires thorough environmental assessments to pinpoint high-risk areas. Collaboration with ornithologists and biologists informs marker and diverter placement, crucial for protecting species like the endangered Great Indian Bustard. While burying power lines remains an ideal but costly option in some areas, complementary measures continue to enhance bird-friendly infrastructure design.

DATA SHEET - VIII
IMPACT OF HUMAN-WILDLIFE CONFLICT ON AVIAN SPECIES IN INDIA

Study Title	Key Findings	Citation
The impact of human-wildlife conflict on biodiversity conservation in India	Highlights the challenges of human-wildlife conflict in India, with significant impact on birds.	[115]
Human-wildlife conflict in India: A review of economic implications and preventive measures	Reviews economic impacts and measures to mitigate human-wildlife conflicts, including those affecting birds.	[115]
Human-wildlife conflict: Issues versus mitigation	Discusses various human-wildlife conflict issues and strategies for mitigation, with reference to bird species.	[116]
Human-wild animal conflict: A threat	Examines human-wildlife conflict and its effects on rural communities, with a focus on bird species.	[117]
Displacement versus co-existence in human-wildlife conflict zones: An overview	Analyzes the displacement and co-existence strategies in human-wildlife conflict zones, affecting birds.	[118]
Human-Wild Animal Conflict	Explores various aspects of human-wildlife conflict and its implications for bird conservation.	[119]

Mapping human–wildlife conflict hotspots in a transboundary landscape, Eastern Himalaya	Identifies conflict hotspots in Eastern Himalaya, with significant impacts on bird species.	[120]
Wildlife-human interactions: From conflict to coexistence in sustainable landscapes	Examines the dynamics of wildlife-human interactions and proposes coexistence strategies.	[121]
Jungle cat (Felis chaus) in farmlands: Potential benefits of coexistence and human-wildlife conflicts in West Bengal, India	Studies the benefits and conflicts of human-wildlife coexistence in agricultural landscapes.	[122]
Human-wildlife conflict and coexistence	Provides an overview of human-wildlife conflict and proposes coexistence strategies, with relevance to birds.	[123]
Compensation payments, procedures, and policies towards human-wildlife conflict management: Insights from India	Reviews compensation policies for human-wildlife conflicts, with a focus on India.	[124]
Human-wildlife conflict in the Mumbai metropolitan region: An empirical study	Investigates the human-wildlife conflict in Mumbai, highlighting bird-related conflicts.	[125]
Human-wildlife conflict in Uttarakhand: Impact, opportunities, and ground-level perspectives with mitigating strategies	Analyzes human-wildlife conflict in Uttarakhand and proposes mitigation strategies.	[126]
Reconciling farming and wild nature: Integrating human-wildlife coexistence into the land-sharing and land-sparing framework	Proposes integrating coexistence strategies into farming practices to mitigate conflicts.	[127]
Indigenous insights on human-wildlife coexistence in southern India	Highlights indigenous practices and insights on human-wildlife coexistence in India.	[128]
Beasts in the garden: Human-wildlife coexistence in India's past and present	Explores historical and contemporary human-wildlife coexistence in India.	[129]

Human-Wildlife Coexistence in the Urban Domain: Promoting Welfare Through Effective Management, Responsibility, and the Recognition of Mutual Interest	Discusses urban human-wildlife coexistence and management strategies.	[130]
Human-wildlife conflict in the roof of the world: Understanding multidimensional perspectives through a systematic review	Systematically reviews human-wildlife conflict in the Himalayan region, affecting birds.	[131]
The evolutionary consequences of human-wildlife conflict in cities	Examines the evolutionary impacts of human-wildlife conflict in urban areas.	[132]
Compensating human-wildlife conflict in protected area communities: Ground-level perspectives from Uttarakhand, India	Analyzes compensation mechanisms for human-wildlife conflicts in Uttarakhand.	[133]

CHAPTER 8

Human-Wildlife Conflict: Sharing Space, Sharing Challenges

1. Crop Raiding and Property Damage: Understanding Bird Behavior

1.1   Food Scarcity and Opportunistic Feeding: Why Birds Target Crops

In the realm of human-wildlife interactions, the phenomenon of birds targeting crops presents a multifaceted challenge deeply intertwined with ecological dynamics and agricultural practices. This issue, prevalent in regions like India where agriculture sustains a significant portion of the population, stems from complex factors ranging from food scarcity to adaptive foraging behaviors. As natural habitats diminish due to deforestation and urbanization, birds increasingly turn to agricultural fields, rich in grains and fruits, for sustenance. This shift is not merely opportunistic but a survival strategy amid dwindling natural food sources.

Seasonal patterns also influence bird behavior, particularly during migratory periods when avian species arrive in India, drawn by the abundance of ripening crops such as rice and millet. This influx coincides with harvest seasons, posing considerable challenges to farmers whose crops become vulnerable to substantial damage. The nutritional allure of crops further compounds the issue, offering birds energy-dense foods and essential nutrients crucial for breeding and survival. Agricultural practices, including monoculture farming and intensive cultivation, inadvertently foster bird reliance on predictable food sources, amplifying crop raiding behaviors through social learning and adaptation.

Climate change exacerbates these dynamics, altering weather patterns and disrupting natural food availability, thereby compelling birds to increasingly rely on cultivated landscapes. Extreme weather events like droughts and floods further drive birds towards agricultural fields as resilient food sources. Addressing these challenges necessitates comprehensive strategies that balance agricultural productivity with wildlife conservation, fostering coexistence through innovative mitigation measures and sustainable farming practices. Such efforts are vital to mitigating conflicts and preserving biodiversity in landscapes where human and avian interests intersect.

1.2   Infrastructure Damage and Nuisance Issues: Mitigating Conflicts

Birds, renowned for their adaptability across diverse environments, frequently clash with human infrastructure, resulting in damage and nuisance concerns. This intersection often leads to significant economic losses and safety hazards, necessitating effective strategies for mitigation. In India, where rapid urbanization transforms landscapes, understanding and addressing avian challenges to infrastructure is crucial. This section delves into the nature of these conflicts, their impact on infrastructure, and diverse mitigation strategies. Birds interact with human-built structures in varied ways, driven by their natural behaviors and urban opportunities. Buildings, bridges, power lines, communication towers, and airports commonly host birds, posing threats such as nesting issues. Species like pigeons, crows, and sparrows favor nesting in building crevices, leading to debris accumulation that clogs gutters and corrodes materials. Communication towers and power lines pose electrocution risks, particularly to large birds like raptors whose wingspans can bridge live wires, causing outages and equipment damage.

Aviation faces unique challenges as birds near runways increase the risk of collisions during takeoffs and landings, necessitating robust bird management for safety. Mitigation strategies employ diverse approaches, including technological solutions, habitat management, and public awareness. Physical deterrents like spikes and nets prevent nesting, while visual methods like reflective tape and predator decoys deter birds temporarily. Auditory deterrents, like distress calls and ultrasonic devices, require careful deployment to avoid noise pollution. Technical solutions for power lines include bird diverters that enhance visibility and redesigns to prevent electrocution. Habitat management modifies surrounding environments to reduce bird attraction, crucial for airports through vegetation and waste management. Public engagement enhances cooperation in bird management efforts, educating about deterrent measures and mutual infrastructure protection. Innovations like laser technology for open spaces and drones for remote monitoring show promise in augmenting these efforts.

2. Retaliatory Killings and Habitat Destruction: A Vicious Cycle

2.1 Traditional Practices and Lack of Awareness: The Roots of Conflict

In India, human-wildlife conflict, particularly detrimental to avian populations, stems largely from entrenched traditional practices and insufficient environmental education. Cultural customs, deeply ingrained and passed through generations, often involve birds in rituals, medicine, or sustenance. Some festivities even include bird capture and sacrifice, reflecting a blend of reverence and inadvertent harm to bird species. Agricultural practices, such as shifting cultivation, historically sustainable at local scales, now threaten habitats crucial for nesting and feeding. As populations grow, demand for land expands, compounding habitat destruction and species decline.

Lack of awareness exacerbates these challenges, with biodiversity's significance often overlooked in conservation efforts. Educational initiatives sporadically address environmental stewardship but rarely localize biodiversity conservation. Socio-economic pressures further drive exploitation of natural resources for survival, including bird hunting and habitat clearance for agriculture and fuel. Modern farming practices, efficient yet chemically intensive, disrupt food chains and expose birds to toxins, impacting reproduction and survival. Urbanization exacerbates habitat fragmentation, disrupting migratory patterns and increasing bird mortality from collisions and pollution. Despite protective legislation, bureaucratic inefficiencies and corruption hinder enforcement, fostering reactive rather than preventive conservation measures. To foster sustainable change, integrating cultural insights with conservation strategies is crucial. Community-led initiatives that respect traditional knowledge empower local stewardship of natural resources, promoting long-term biodiversity conservation aligned with cultural values.

2.2 Habitat Loss and Reduced Food Availability: A Cycle of Displacement and Conflict

The nexus between habitat loss and dwindling food resources constitutes a pivotal catalyst of human-wildlife conflict in India, significantly impacting avian populations. As natural landscapes succumb to encroachment and destruction, birds confront displacement, grappling to secure suitable grounds for nesting, foraging, and breeding. This displacement precipitates closer proximity with human settlements, amplifying conflicts and perpetuating a precarious cycle that imperils both avian and human communities. To unravel this intricate issue, a comprehensive exploration of the multifaceted origins, repercussions of habitat loss, and implications for food availability is indispensable.

Habitat depletion in India primarily stems from agricultural expansion, urbanization, deforestation, and infrastructure development. Escalating population growth and economic demands necessitate the conversion of forests, grasslands, wetlands, and other habitats into farmlands, residential areas, and industrial zones. Particularly pronounced in biodiversity hotspots such as the Western Ghats, Eastern Himalayas, and Terai Arc, this transformation disrupts ecosystem equilibrium, severely compromising birds' access to vital resources.

Agricultural expansion, while vital for sustenance, encroaches upon habitats crucial for diverse bird species. Traditional farming methods, once harmonious with wildlife, have given way to intensive monoculture, eradicating hedgerows, wetlands, and other microhabitats pivotal for avian shelter and sustenance. Concurrently, the widespread use of chemical pesticides and fertilizers decimates insect populations-a staple food source for many birds-drastically reducing food availability and necessitating broader foraging ranges. Urban sprawl and infrastructure projects pose additional threats by clearing extensive swathes of natural terrain, fragmenting contiguous habitats into isolated patches. Such fragmentation severely limits nesting sites and foraging grounds, posing grave challenges for migratory species dependent on expansive, unbroken habitats. Deforestation, driven by logging, mining, and land conversion, compounds habitat loss, dismantling critical ecosystems and depriving specialized bird species of essential tree-dependent habitats.

Wetlands, pivotal for diverse bird species including waterfowl and migratory birds, face drainage and conversion to agricultural and urban purposes, compromising abundant food sources and secure nesting sites. This displacement compels birds into human-dominated landscapes in pursuit of sustenance, escalating conflicts as birds raid crops, prompting retaliatory measures from farmers. Moreover, urban environments offer inadequate food diversity and nesting opportunities, posing risks such as collisions, pollution, and malnutrition among birds. Anthropogenic food sources like garbage dumps alter natural behaviors, impacting ecological dynamics and long-term biodiversity.

4. Beyond Coexistence: Fostering Positive Human-Bird Relationships

4.1 The Value of Birdwatching: Connecting with Nature and Promoting Conservation

Birdwatching, a globally cherished recreational pursuit, holds profound significance in cultivating a profound connection with the natural world and advancing conservation efforts. Beyond simple observation, this activity immerses enthusiasts in avian diversity, fostering a deep appreciation for nature's intricacies. By engaging in birdwatching, individuals not only enrich their own well-being but also contribute to broader environmental conservation endeavors. The practice of birdwatching promotes mindfulness and an intimate engagement with nature. Enthusiasts attune their senses to subtle bird behaviors, plumage nuances, and melodious songs, thereby deepening their understanding of local ecosystems. This heightened awareness often translates into a profound respect for the natural environment and a personal commitment to its preservation. Research indicates that time spent in nature, such as through birdwatching, alleviates stress, enhances mental health, and promotes overall well-being, underscoring its dual role as leisure pursuit and therapeutic endeavor.

Additionally, birdwatching fosters a sense of community among its devotees. Through clubs, group outings, and birding festivals, enthusiasts exchange knowledge, sightings, and experiences, forming networks dedicated to bird conservation and environmental stewardship. Citizen science initiatives like the Audubon Society's Christmas Bird Count and Cornell Lab of Ornithology's eBird rely on data collected by birdwatchers. This information is critical for tracking bird populations, studying migration patterns, and identifying conservation priorities.

A pivotal contribution of birdwatching lies in its role as a data source for scientific research and policy formulation. Citizen scientists provide essential data on bird populations and habitats, enriching our understanding of avian ecology and informing conservation strategies. This collaboration between amateur birdwatchers and professional ornithologists has been instrumental in identifying declining species and advocating for protective measures. Furthermore, birdwatching supports conservation through economic avenues such as avitourism. Birdwatching tourism attracts enthusiasts to natural reserves and parks, generating revenue that funds conservation projects. Many regions have leveraged this interest by developing birdwatching trails, establishing sanctuaries, and promoting eco-friendly accommodations. This sustainable tourism model not only bolsters local economies but also raises awareness about the importance of preserving bird habitats.

4.2 Economic Benefits of Birdwatching: Ecotourism and Sustainable Wildlife Management

Birdwatching exerts a profound economic influence extending well beyond the tourism sector. It resonates across diverse industries, encompassing hospitality, transportation, and local commerce. As birdwatchers seek accommodation, sustenance, transport, and expert guidance, they fuel revenue streams for hotels, eateries, tour operators, and indigenous artisans. This influx not only spawns employment opportunities but also catalyzes economic vitality within these regions. Small enterprises, such as local crafts shops and food vendors, directly profit from heightened foot traffic, thereby fostering grassroots entrepreneurship and sustainable economic growth.

Central to the economic impact of birdwatching is the surge in job creation. Ecotourism-related vocations-bird guides, conservationists, park wardens, and hospitality personnel-provide vital livelihoods, especially in rural and secluded locales. Training residents as bird guides capitalizes on their native environmental knowledge while ensuring income generation. Such community-centered approaches empower local populations and equitably distribute the economic dividends of ecotourism. Infrastructure development tailored for birdwatchers further augments economic momentum. Investments in eco-lodges, observation hides, trails, and visitor centers not only enrich visitor experiences but also extend tourist stays, amplifying per-visitor spending. Enhanced infrastructure can attract diverse forms of nature-based tourism, compounding economic benefits. Governments and private investors increasingly acknowledge birdwatching's potential as a sustainable economic activity, prompting heightened funding and backing for ecotourism initiatives.

Crucially, birdwatching advances sustainable wildlife stewardship by prioritizing habitat conservation. Economic incentives linked to birdwatching tourism incentivize the preservation of forests, wetlands, grasslands, and other critical avian habitats. Communities and governments alike are incentivized to uphold these areas, ensuring robust conservation efforts. Revenues from ecotourism are often reinvested in conservation endeavors-habitat restoration, anti-poaching measures, and biodiversity monitoring-bolstering environmental resilience. Furthermore, birdwatching tourism fosters community-led conservation initiatives. Engaging local communities in conservation ensures direct benefits from safeguarding natural resources. Programs like participatory forest management and eco-development initiatives not only protect bird habitats but also provide alternative livelihoods, mitigating human-wildlife conflicts. By intertwining economic incentives with conservation goals, birdwatching cultivates a sustainable framework for wildlife management, promoting harmonious coexistence between people and avifauna.

5. Finding Solutions: Strategies for Effective Human-Wildlife Conflict Management

5.1 Utilizing Non-lethal Deterrents: Protecting Crops and Minimizing Bird Mortality

Utilizing non-lethal methods to protect crops while minimizing bird mortality is pivotal in managing human-wildlife conflicts, particularly in agricultural landscapes where birds and farmers vie for resources. This approach not only safeguards avian biodiversity but also promotes sustainable agricultural practices, fostering a harmonious coexistence. Effective implementation of non-lethal deterrents hinges upon a nuanced grasp of bird behavior, innovative technologies, and community involvement, underscoring the complexity and potential of this strategy.

Birds pose a significant threat to crops, impacting farmers' livelihoods by damaging cereals, fruits, vegetables, and aquaculture products like fish. Species such as parrots, sparrows, and crows are frequent culprits, causing reduced yields and financial strain. Traditional responses to this issue, including lethal methods such as shooting and poisoning, not only harm bird populations but disrupt ecosystems with unintended consequences. Non-lethal deterrents offer a humane and ecologically sound alternative.

Visual scare devices represent one of the most effective non-lethal methods. Utilizing materials like Mylar reflective tape creates light flashes and sounds in the wind, deterring birds from approaching crops. Scarecrows, enhanced with motion or sound, emulate human presence effectively. Predator models such as plastic owls strategically placed in fields also discourage bird incursions. Innovative technologies like drones equipped with bird-like features or programmed to mimic predator behaviors patrol agricultural areas, adapting actively to bird behavior. This relatively new technology has shown promise in field trials due to its mobility and adaptability. Auditory deterrents emit distressing sounds for birds, including predator calls and ultrasonic devices. While effective, static auditory deterrents require variation to prevent habituation. Chemical repellents like methyl anthranilate, derived from grapes, and capsaicin from chili peppers, provide taste or odor aversions without harming birds or humans. Habitat modification, such as removing roosting sites and planting less attractive vegetation near crops, can significantly mitigate bird-related damage over the long term. Biological controls, encouraging natural predators like raptors through perches or nesting boxes, help maintain ecological balance by regulating bird populations.

5.2 Education and Community Engagement: Building Understanding and Collaboration

Education and community engagement are pivotal in mitigating human-wildlife conflicts involving birds in India. These approaches foster understanding, promote coexistence, and develop collaborative solutions. Educating communities about the ecological importance of birds and involving them in conservation efforts can lead to a more harmonious relationship benefiting both humans and wildlife. Birds serve critical roles in ecosystems as pollinators, seed dispersers, and natural pest controllers, contributing to biodiversity and ecosystem health. However, human activities like agriculture and urbanization often lead to habitat loss and increased encounters between birds and people, resulting in conflicts such as crop damage and safety concerns. Education and engagement are key to addressing these issues by raising awareness and promoting practices that reduce conflict.

Effective education programs are essential, tailored to diverse audiences including farmers, school children, urban residents, and policymakers. For farmers, highlighting birds' benefits in pest control and crop yield enhancement can encourage adoption of bird-friendly practices. Integrating bird conservation into school curricula can inspire stewardship among students through activities like birdwatching and nature lessons. Urban communities also play a crucial role, with cities serving as important bird habitats. Education programs can focus on creating bird-friendly environments through native plantings and reduced pesticide use. Involving residents in citizen science projects enhances community involvement and supports conservation efforts.

Engaging communities requires building trust and fostering collaboration, ensuring participation in decision-making processes. Community-based initiatives like bird monitoring empower residents, integrating local knowledge and enhancing project success. Collaborative approaches involving farmers, local leaders, and conservationists are particularly effective in rural areas, where conflicts are more pronounced. Clear, culturally sensitive communication is vital, utilizing local languages and media to enhance message impact. Visual aids and digital platforms can make information accessible and engaging, fostering a broader understanding and support for bird conservation efforts.

6. The Peril of Persistent Toxins: Understanding Biomagnification

6.1   The Case of DDT: A Widespread Pesticide with Devastating Effects

DDT, known as dichlorodiphenyltrichloroethane, emerged as a revolutionary pesticide during World War II, celebrated for its effectiveness in combating diseases like malaria and protecting crops. This accolade earned its discoverer, Paul Hermann Müller, the Nobel Prize in 1948. However, DDT's durability and broad-spectrum properties also posed significant environmental risks, notably through biomagnification-a process where its concentration escalates up the food chain. Applied to fields and waterways, DDT entered plants and small organisms, accumulating as it progressed through successive trophic levels. At the apex, predators such as birds accumulated toxic levels, triggering profound consequences. Birds, particularly raptors like the bald eagle and peregrine falcon, bore the brunt of DDT's impact. The pesticide interfered with calcium metabolism, resulting in eggshell thinning and increased nest failures. By the 1960s, populations of peregrine falcons across North America plummeted, their eggshells becoming dangerously fragile. Aquatic birds, reliant on fish contaminated by DDT, faced similar reproductive struggles, exacerbating ecological imbalances in their habitats.

Beyond its ecological toll, DDT's pervasive use in public health initiatives and household products caused widespread contamination of soil, water, and air globally. Rachel Carson's influential book, "Silent Spring," raised public awareness about the pesticide's environmental hazards, catalyzing stricter regulations and eventual bans in many countries by 1972. Yet, DDT's persistence in the environment continues to pose challenges, as evidenced by ongoing residues found in ecosystems worldwide, including in various regions of India where its use was historically extensive in malaria control efforts. The legacy of DDT serves as a stark reminder of the complex interplay between human health, environmental stewardship, and wildlife conservation, underscoring the enduring importance of informed, sustainable pest management practices in safeguarding ecosystems for future generations.

Reference

1.   Birdsofindia.org. *INDIAN BIRDS IN THE IUCN RED LIST.* 2024 26-06-2024]; Available from: https://www.birdsofindia.org/IUCN-Red-List.

2.   Sirur, S. *Habitat and food loss, changing ecosystems see 60% of India's bird population decline.* 2023   14-04-2024];   Available   from: https://scroll.in/article/1055136/habitat-and-food-loss-changing-ecosystems-see-60-of-indias-bird-population-decline.

3.   MISHRA, I. *Birds living in open habitat seeing declining trend, large number of common species in trouble: report.* 2023   12-02-2024]; Available from: read://https_www.thehindu.com/?url=https%3A%2F%2Fwww.thehindu.com%2Fsci-tech%2Fenergy-and-environment%2Fbirds-living-in-open-habitat-seeing-declining-trend-large-number-of-common-species-in-trouble-report%2Farticle67236248.ece.

4.   Abraham, B. *State of India's Birds 2023: Conservation Of 178 Species Should Be Highly Prioritised, Says New Study.* 2023   [cited 27-01-2024; Available from: https://www.indiatimes.com/amp/news/india/state-of-indias-birds-2023-conservation-of-178-bird-species-in-india-should-be-prioritised-613188.html.

5.   Padma, T.V. *Land use changes are driving Himalayan forest bird loss.* 2021 12-01-2023]; Available from: https://india.mongabay.com/2021/03/land-use-changes-driving-himalayan-forest-bird-loss/.

6.   BAVADAM, L. *India's declining birdlife.* 2020 23-04-2023]; Available from: https://frontline.thehindu.com/environment/conservation/article31038561.ece.

7.   JOHN P. CROXALL, S.H.M.B., BEN LASCELLES, ALISON J. STATTERSFIELD, BEN SULLIVAN, ANDY SYMESl, PHIL TAYLOR, *Seabird conservation status, threats and priority actions: a global assessment.* Cambridge University Press, 2012.

8.   Singh, B.B. and A.A. Gajadhar, *Role of India's wildlife in the emergence and re-emergence of zoonotic pathogens, risk factors and public health implications.* Acta Tropica, 2014. **138**: p. 67-77.

9.   Velho, N., *Conservation challenges of wet-tropical nature reserves in north-east India.* 2015, James Cook University.

10.   Nalavade, S.B., *Retreating Wild Mammals of Pune Urban Area.* Journal of Ecological Society, 2001. **13**(1): p. 74-80.

11.   University, D. *Birds Face Extinction Risk Due To Human Activities.* 2006 04-01-2024];   Available   from: https://news.mongabay.com/2006/07/birds-face-extinction-risk-due-to-human-activities/.

12.   Karjee, R., et al., *Bird assemblages in a peri-urban landscape in eastern India.* Birds, 2022. **3**(4): p. 383-401.

13.   Zhang, Y., et al., *The relationship between landscape construction and bird diversity: A bibliometric analysis.* International Journal of Environmental Research and Public Health, 2023. **20**(5): p. 4551.

14. Filloy, J., G.A. Zurita, and M.I. Bellocq, *Bird diversity in urban ecosystems: the role of the biome and land use along urbanization gradients.* Ecosystems, 2019. **22**: p. 213-227.

15. Baral, H., J.B. Giri, and M.Z. Virani, *On the decline of Oriental White-backed Vultures Gyps bengalensis in lowland Nepal.* Raptors Worldwide. Berlin and Budapest: World Working Group on Birds of Prey and Owls and MME/Birdlife Hungary, 2004: p. 215-219.

16. Raman, T.S., *Effects of habitat structure and adjacent habitats on birds in tropical rainforest fragments and shaded plantations in the Western Ghats, India.* Forest diversity and management, 2006: p. 517-547.

17. Mandal, J. and T. Shankar Raman, *Shifting agriculture supports more tropical forest birds than oil palm or teak plantations in Mizoram, northeast India.* The Condor: Ornithological Applications, 2016. **118**(2): p. 345-359.

18. Jayapal, R., Q. Qureshi, and R. Chellam, *Importance of forest structure versus floristics to composition of avian assemblages in tropical deciduous forests of Central Highlands, India.* Forest Ecology and Management, 2009. **257**(11): p. 2287-2295.

19. Sandilyan, S., et al., *Impacts of invasive alien species on island ecosystems of India with special reference to Andaman group of islands-National Biodiversity Authority.* 2018, Chennai.

20. Weller, M.W., *Wetland birds: habitat resources and conservation implications.* 1999: Cambridge University Press.

21. Bhagwat, S.A., et al., *A landscape approach to biodiversity conservation of sacred groves in the Western Ghats of India.* Conservation Biology, 2005. **19**(6): p. 1853-1862.

22. Anthony, F.M. and G. Tiwari, *Anthropogenic noise reduces bird species richness and diversity along a Rur-urban gradient: A case study from a city in central India during nationwide lockdown amid COVID-19.* Journal of Biodiversity and Environmental Sciences| JBES, 2022. **20**(1): p. 1-9.

23. Roller, H.F., *Amazonian routes: indigenous mobility and colonial communities in northern Brazil.* 2014: Stanford University Press.

24. Rao, A.S.S., *Modeling the rapid spread of avian influenza (H5N1) in India.* Mathematical Biosciences & Engineering, 2008. **5**(3): p. 523-537.

25. Trivedi, P. and V. Soni, *Significant bird records and local extinctions in Purna and Ratanmahal Wildlife Sanctuaries, Gujarat, India.* Forktail, 2006. **22**: p. 39.

26. Anil, M., K. Kumari, and S. Wate, *Loss of biodiversity and conservation strategies: an outlook of Indian scenario.* Asian Journal of Conservation Biology, 2014. **3**(2): p. 105-114.

27. Kumar, A. and A. Verma, *Biodiversity loss and its Ecological impact in India.* International Journal on Biological Sciences, 2017. **8**(2): p. 156-160.

28. Adhurya, S., S. Adhurya, and U.S. Roy, *Rapid degradation of wetlands and its impact on avifauna: A case study from Ambuja Wetland, West Bengal, India.* Indian Birds, 2019. **15**(2): p. 43-48.

29.   Balachandran, S., *Decline of coastal birds along the south-east coast of India.* Conservation and Valuation of Marine Biodiversity, 2007. **41**: p. 41.

30.   Shahabuddin, G., et al., *Decline in forest bird species and guilds due to land use change in the Western Himalaya.* Global Ecology and Conservation, 2021. **25**: p. e01447.

31.   Vergara-Tabares, D.L., et al., *Global trends of habitat destruction and consequences for parrot conservation.* Global Change Biology, 2020. **26**(8): p. 4251-4262.

32.   Kandel, P., et al., *Birds of the Kangchenjunga Landscape, the Eastern Himalaya: status, threats and implications for conservation.* Avian Research, 2018. **9**: p. 1-13.

33.   Tan, Y.-L., et al., *Habitat change and biodiversity loss in South and Southeast Asian countries.* Environmental Science and Pollution Research, 2022. **29**(42): p. 63260-63276.

34.   Guthula, V.B., et al., *Biodiversity significance of small habitat patches: More than half of Indian bird species are in academic campuses.* Landscape and Urban Planning, 2022. **228**: p. 104552.

35.   Pandit, M., et al., *Unreported yet massive deforestation driving loss of endemic biodiversity in Indian Himalaya.* Biodiversity and Conservation, 2007. **16**: p. 153-163.

36.   Dinda, S.C., et al., *Bird Species diversity from the Southern West part of West Bengal, India.* International Journal of clinical and Medical Case Reports, 2023. **2**(5).

37.   Byju, H., et al., *Transitioning Wintering Shorebirds to Agroecosystem: A Thorough Evaluation of Habitat Selection and Conservation Concern.* Diversity, 2023. **16**(1): p. 23.

38.   Ashwin, C.P., et al., *Raptors and linear infrastructure in Chhattisgarh, India: species composition and conservation concern.* Ornis Hungarica, 2023. **31**(2): p. 1-12.

39.   Kumar, M., A. Kumar, and S.K. Bhardwaj, *Diversity, composition and conservation status of avian fauna in the forest and the wetland sites of Hastinapur wildlife sanctuary, India.* Environment Conservation Journal, 2023. **24**(2): p. 334-342.

40.   MISHRA, I. *Birds living in open habitat seeing declining trend, large number of common species in trouble: report.* 2023 17-03-2024]; Available from: https://www.thehindu.com/sci-tech/energy-and-environment/birds-living-in-open-habitat-seeing-declining-trend-large-number-of-common-species-in-trouble-report/article67236248.ece.

41.   Chauhan, A. *Bird species plummeting in India, says new report: What are the major threats to them?* 2023 [cited 20-02-2024; Available from: https://indianexpress.com/article/explained/threats-bird-species-india-8911046/lite/.

42.   Nandi, J. *48% of bird species declining globally; 50% declining strongly in India.* 2022 11-01-2024]; Available from: https://www.hindustantimes.com/india-news/48-of-bird-species-declining-globally-50-declining-strongly-in-India-101652034320021.html.

43. DAVIS, T.T. *Logging and Habitat Degradation: Conserving Wildlife*. 2023 29-01-2024]; Available from: https://wildlife-conservation.org/logging/.

44. Saha, D.C. and P.K. Padhy, *Effect of air and noise pollution on species diversity and population density of forest birds at Lalpahari, West Bengal, India*. Science of the Total Environment, 2011. **409**(24): p. 5328-5336.

45. Newman, J.R. and R. Schreiber, *Air pollution and wildlife toxicology: An overlooked problem*. Environmental Toxicology and Chemistry: An International Journal, 1988. **7**(5): p. 381-390.

46. Sullivan, K.D. *Air pollution is threatening birds' health*. 2017 05-04-2024]; Available from: https://www.labroots.com/trending/earth-and-the-environment/6656/air-pollution-threatening-birds-health.

47. Pati, I. *Stricken by smog: Toxic air is choking birds too*. 2023 25-04-2024]; Available from: https://timesofindia.indiatimes.com/city/gurgaon/stricken-by-smog-toxic-air-is-choking-birds-too/articleshow/105505806.cms.

48. Shandilya, P. *Migratory birds missing as pollution levels rise in Delhi NCR*. 2019 31-01-2024]; Available from: https://www.indiatoday.in/india/story/migratory-birds-missing-as-pollution-levels-rise-in-delhi-ncr-1610148-2019-10-17.

49. Richard, F.-J., et al., *Warning on nine pollutants and their effects on avian communities*. Global Ecology and Conservation, 2021. **32**: p. e01898.

50. Deomurari, A., et al., *Projected shifts in bird distribution in India under climate change*. Diversity, 2023. **15**(3): p. 404.

51. Sparkle, T. *10 Ways Air Pollution Impacts Birds: Understanding the Ecological Consequences*. 2024 24-05-2024]; Available from: https://www.onegreenplanet.org/animals/10-ways-air-pollution-impacts-birds-understanding-the-ecological-consequences/.

52. Vashishtha, A. *Birds flee or die in polluted NCR*. 2010 17-01-2024]; Available from: https://www.indiatoday.in/india/north/story/birds-flee-or-die-in-polluted-ncr-65197-2010-01-17.

53. Naroju, S. *12 Unimaginable Effects of Air Pollution on Birds*. 2023 14-04-2024]; Available from: https://www.riddlelife.com/effects-of-air-pollution-on-birds/.

54. Raghvendra Mishra, L.S., S. Shukla, *Impacts of Artificial Lighting on Avian Biodiversity: A Case Study of Udaipur (Rajasthan), India*. Environmental Science, Biology, 2024(21-04-2024).

55. Patel, K., et al. *Samachar: print news media on air pollution in India*. in *Proceedings of the 5th ACM SIGCAS/SIGCHI Conference on Computing and Sustainable Societies*. 2022.

56. Bala, M., A. Sharma, and G. Sharma, *Spatial Variation of Trace Metals Between Industrial and Rural Dwelling Birds of India*. Nature Environment & Pollution Technology, 2021. **20**.

57. Sullivan, K.D. *Air pollution is threatening birds' health*. 2017 01-04-2024]; Available from: https://www.labroots.com/trending/earth-and-the-environment/6656/air-pollution-threatening-birds-health.

58.   Taylor, L., C. Taylor, and A. Davis, *The impact of urbanisation on avian species: The inextricable link between people and birds.* Urban Ecosystems, 2013. **16**: p. 481-498.

59.   NSF. *Noise and light pollution affect breeding habits in birds.* 2020 18-05-2024]; Available from: https://new.nsf.gov/news/noise-light-pollution-affect-breeding-habits-birds.

60.   Ghosh, S. *Light pollution on the rise in India: Study.* 2019 21-03-2024]; Available from: https://india.mongabay.com/2019/01/light-pollution-on-the-rise-in-india-study/.

61.   Walsh, M.G., et al., *A biogeographical description of the wild waterbird species associated with high-risk landscapes of Japanese encephalitis virus in India.* Transboundary and Emerging Diseases, 2022. **69**(5): p. e3015-e3023.

62.   Gopinath, R., et al., *Impact of chaotic urbanisation on Bengaluru's (India) urban avian diversity.* Transylvanian Review of Systematical and Ecological Research, 2021. **23**(1): p. 81-94.

63.   Gawande, U., et al., *EFFECTS OF AMBIENT AIR POLLUTION ON RESPIRATORY HEALTH OF CHILDREN: FINDINGS FROM A CROSS-SECTIONAL STUDY IN CHANDRAPUR, MAHARASHTRA, INDIA.* International Journal of Current Research and Review, 2016. **8**(2): p. 36.

64.   O'Hanlon, N. *Birds and pollution.* 2021 14-02-2024]; Available from: https://www.bto.org/understanding-birds/articles/birds-and-pollution.

65.   Biswas, G., et al., *Migratory Birds in Peril: Unravelling the Impact of Climate Change.* A Basic Overview of Environment and Sustainable Development [Volume: 2], 2023: p. 35.

66.   Kannan, R. and D.A. James, *Effects of climate change on global biodiversity: a review of key literature.* Tropical Ecology, 2009. **50**(1): p. 31.

67.   Srinivasan, U. and D.S. Wilcove, *Interactive impacts of climate change and land-use change on the demography of montane birds.* Ecology, 2021. **102**(1): p. e03223.

68.   Surasinghe, T., *The effects of climate change on global wildlife and terrestrial ecosystems.* TAPROBANICA: The Journal of Asian Biodiversity, 2011. **2**(1).

69.   Sauve, D., V.L. Friesen, and A. Charmantier, *The effects of weather on avian growth and implications for adaptation to climate change.* Frontiers in Ecology and Evolution, 2021. **9**: p. 569741.

70.   Chambers, L.E., L. Hughes, and M.A. Weston, *Climate change and its impact on Australia's avifauna.* Emu-Austral Ornithology, 2005. **105**(1): p. 1-20.

71.   Zuckerberg, B., *Birds and climate change: Impacts and conservation responses.* The Condor: Ornithological Applications, 2017. **119**(1): p. 170-171.

72.   Dandotiya, B. and H.K. Sharma, *Climate change and its impact on terrestrial ecosystems,* in *Research Anthology on Environmental and Societal Impacts of Climate Change.* 2022, IGI Global. p. 88-101.

73.   Kumar, N., *Ecological impacts of poultry waste on urban raptors: conflicts, diseases, and climate change implications amidst pandemic threats.* bioRxiv, 2023: p. 2023.07. 13.546415.

74.   Stewart, P.S., et al., *Global impacts of climate change on avian functional diversity.* Ecology Letters, 2022. **25**(3): p. 673-685.

75.   Singh, H., et al., *Climate change shifts the habitat suitability of range-restricted bird species (Catreus wallichii) in the Himalayan ecosystem: evidence from the Indian Himalayan Ecosystem.* 2022.

76.   Carey, C., *The impacts of climate change on the annual cycles of birds.* Philosophical Transactions of the Royal Society B: Biological Sciences, 2009. **364**(1534): p. 3321-3330.

77.   Patankar, S., et al., *Which traits influence bird survival in the city? A review.* Land, 2021. **10**(2): p. 92.

78.   Sundar, K.G., *Agricultural intensification, rainfall patterns, and large waterbird breeding success in the extensively cultivated landscape of Uttar Pradesh, India.* Biological Conservation, 2011. **144**(12): p. 3055-3063.

79.   Dahal, N., S. Lamichhaney, and S. Kumar, *Climate change impacts on Himalayan biodiversity: evidence-based perception and current approaches to evaluate threats under climate change.* Journal of the Indian Institute of Science, 2021. **101**(2): p. 195-210.

80.   Ishtiaq, F., *Ecology and evolution of avian malaria: implications of land use changes and climate change on disease dynamics.* Journal of the Indian Institute of Science, 2021. **101**(2): p. 213-225.

81.   Bharadwaj, A., R. Chanda, and U. Srinivasan, *Abiotic niche predictors of long-term trends in body mass and survival of Eastern Himalayan birds.* bioRxiv, 2022: p. 2022.08. 25.505219.

82.   D'Cruze, N., et al., *A star attraction: The illegal trade in Indian Star Tortoises.* Nature Conservation, 2015. **13**: p. 1-19.

83.   Poonia, A., et al., *Trends in CITES listed bird's trade in South Asian countries in view of evolution of Indian laws during last four decades.* International Journal of Ecological Economics and Statistics, 2022. **43**(9): p. 115.

84.   D'Cruze, N., et al., *Trading tactics: Time to rethink the global trade in wildlife.* Animals, 2020. **10**(12): p. 2456.

85.   Jayakrishnan, R., *An Analysis of Criminal Laws against Poaching Animals and Wildlife Trafficking.* Issue 2 Indian JL & Legal Rsch., 2023. **5**: p. 1.

86.   Dutta, H., *Illegal avian and reptilian pets: Global perspectives and challenges.* Cuadernos de Biodiversidad, 2023(65): p. 4-22.

87.   Kumawat, S., *A Study on Wildlife Trafficking and the Issue of Poaching: The Law and Judicial Outlook.* Issue 1 Indian JL & Legal Rsch., 2023. **5**: p. 1.

88.   Bhattacharyya, D., *Market for Animal Body Parts and Tiger Poaching: National Environmental Laws to Counter This Scenery.* Jus Corpus LJ, 2021. **2**: p. 121.

89. Uprety, Y., et al., *Illegal wildlife trade is threatening conservation in the transboundary landscape of Western Himalaya.* Journal for Nature Conservation, 2021. **59**: p. 125952.

90. Rana, A.K. and N. Kumar, *Current wildlife crime (Indian scenario): major challenges and prevention approaches.* Biodiversity and Conservation, 2023. **32**(5): p. 1473-1491.

91. Singh, R., J. Sethy, and D. Chatrath, *TRENDS AND PATTERNS OF ILLEGAL WILDLIFE HUNTING AND TRADING IN UTTAR PRADESH, INDIA.* International Journal of Conservation Science, 2023. **14**(1).

92. Puri, G., et al., *Poaching and Illegal Trade of Wildlife: What Do the Media Say for the Nepali-Chinese and Nepali-Indian Border?* Hindu Kush-Himalaya Watersheds Downhill: Landscape Ecology and Conservation Perspectives, 2020: p. 695-716.

93. Mitra, S., *A Critical Analysis on the Impact of Poaching of Animals on Environment and the Laws Prohibiting It in India.* Issue 2 Int'l JL Mgmt. & Human., 2023. **6**: p. 1271.

94. Chawla, M.M., et al., *Do wildlife crimes against less charismatic species go unnoticed? A case study of Golden Jackal Canis aureus Linnaeus, 1758 poaching and trade in India.* Journal of Threatened Taxa, 2020. **12**: p. 15407-15413.

95. Clarke, R.V. and R.A. de By, *Poaching, habitat loss and the decline of neotropical parrots: A comparative spatial analysis.* Journal of Experimental Criminology, 2013. **9**: p. 333-353.

96. Becerra, S., J. Marinero, and C.E. Borghi, *Poaching and illegal wildlife trade in western Argentina.* Ethnobiology and Conservation, 2022. **11**.

97. Conrad, K., *Trade bans: a perfect storm for poaching?* Tropical Conservation Science, 2012. **5**(3): p. 245-254.

98. Gomez, L., et al., *An analysis of the illegal bear trade in India.* Global Ecology and Conservation, 2021. **27**: p. e01552.

99. Niraj, S.K., *Sustainable development, poaching, and illegal wildlife trade in India.* 2009: The University of Arizona.

100. Van Uhm, D.P., *The illegal wildlife trade: Inside the world of poachers, smugglers and traders.* Vol. 15. 2016: Springer.

101. Raman, T.S., *Framing ecologically sound policy on linear intrusions affecting wildlife habitats.* Nature Conservation Foundation, Mysuru, India, 2011.

102. Sur, S., P.K. Saikia, and M.K. Saikia, *Speed thrills but kills: A case study on seasonal variation in roadkill mortality on National highway 715 (new) in Kaziranga-Karbi Anglong Landscape, Assam, India.* Nature Conservation, 2022(47).

103. Rao, S. and V.K. Koli, *Edge effect of busy high traffic roads on the nest site selection of birds inside the city area: Guild response.* Transportation Research Part D: Transport and Environment, 2017. **51**: p. 94-101.

104. Tejera, G., et al., *Wildlife-vehicle collisions in Lanzarote biosphere reserve, Canary Islands.* PLoS One, 2018. **13**(3): p. e0192731.

105. Saxena, A., et al., *Integrating large mammal behaviour and traffic flow to determine traversability of roads with heterogeneous traffic on a Central Indian Highway.* Scientific reports, 2020. **10**(1): p. 18888.

106. Kumara, H.N., et al., *Responses of birds and mammals to long-established wind farms in India.* Scientific reports, 2022. **12**(1): p. 1339.

107. Joshi, R. and A. Dixit, *WILDLIFE MORTALITY ON NATIONAL HIGHWAY 72 AND 74 ACROSS THE RAJAJI NATIONAL PARK AND THE HARIDWAR CONSERVATION AREA, NORTH INDIA.* International Journal of Conservation Science, 2012. **3**(2).

108. Rajvanshi, A., et al., *Roads, sensitive habitats and wildlife: environmental guideline for India and South Asia.* 2001: Wildlife Intstitute of India.

109. Van Der Ree, R., D.J. Smith, and C. Grilo, *The ecological effects of linear infrastructure and traffic: challenges and opportunities of rapid global growth.* Handbook of road ecology, 2015: p. 1-9.

110. Travers, M.S., *Reducing collisions with structures*, in *Conservation of Marine Birds.* 2023, Elsevier. p. 379-401.

111. Seiler, A. and J.O. Helldin, *Mortality in wildlife due to transportation*, in *The ecology of transportation: Managing mobility for the environment.* 2006, Springer. p. 165-189.

112. Seewagen, C. and C. Sheppard, *Bird collisions with glass: an annotated bibliography.* American Bird Conservancy, Washington, 2017.

113. Bishop, C.A. and J.M. Brogan, *Estimates of Avian Mortality Attributed to Vehicle Collisions in Canada Estimation de la mortalité aviaire attribuable aux collisions automobiles au Canada.* Avian Conservation and Ecology, 2013. **8**(2): p. 2.

114. Betleja, J., et al., *Birds crossing over roads: species, flight heights and infrastructure use.* European Journal of Ecology, 2020. **6**(2).

115. Padmakumar, V. and M. Shanthakumar, *The impact of human-wildlife conflict on biodiversity conservation in India.* J. Entomol. Zool. Stud, 2023. **11**(3): p. 107-110.

116. Anwar, R., H.S. Saralch, and S. Kumar, *Human-wildlife conflict: issues versus mitigation.* Indian For, 2015. **141**(12): p. 1305-1314.

117. Soni, A., et al., *Human-wild animal conflict: A threat.* INDiAN FARmER: p. 530.

118. Rai, J., *Displacement versus co-existence in human-wildlife conflict zones: An overview.* J. Geogr. Environ. Earth Sci. Int, 2019: p. 1-16.

119. Somu, Y. and S. Palanisamy, *Human-Wild Animal Conflict*, in *Animal Welfare-New Insights.* 2022, IntechOpen.

120. Sharma, P., et al., *Mapping human–wildlife conflict hotspots in a transboundary landscape, Eastern Himalaya.* Global Ecology and Conservation, 2020. **24**: p. e01284.

121. Thomassen, J., J.D. Linnell, and K. Skogen, *Wildlife-human interactions: from conflict to coexistence in sustainable landscapes.* NINA rapport, 2011.

122. Mahato, S., et al., *Jungle cat (Felis chaus) in farmlands: potential benefits of coexistence and human-wildlife conflicts in West Bengal, India.* Ethology Ecology & Evolution, 2023. **35**(5): p. 568-583.

123. Nyhus, P.J., *Human-wildlife conflict and coexistence.* Annual review of environment and resources, 2016. **41**(1): p. 143-171.

124. Karanth, K.K., S. Gupta, and A. Vanamamalai, *Compensation payments, procedures and policies towards human-wildlife conflict management: Insights from India.* Biological Conservation, 2018. **227**: p. 383-389.

125. Sharma, D. and P. Sinha, *Human-wildlife conflict in the mumbai metropolitan region-an empirical study.* Urban Ecology and Global Climate Change, 2022: p. 250-272.

126. Meena, D., *Human-wildlife conflict in Uttarakhand: Impact, opportunities and ground level perspectives with mitigating strategies.* Proceedings of the International Academy of Ecology and Environmental Sciences, 2021. **11**(3): p. 84.

127. Crespin, S.J. and J.A. Simonetti, *Reconciling farming and wild nature: Integrating human-wildlife coexistence into the land-sharing and land-sparing framework.* Ambio, 2019. **48**: p. 131-138.

128. Jolly, H., et al., *Indigenous insights on human-wildlife coexistence in southern India.* Conservation Biology, 2022. **36**(6): p. e13981.

129. Oommen, M.A., *Beasts in the garden: human-wildlife coexistence in India's past and present.* Frontiers in Conservation Science, 2021. **2**: p. 703432.

130. Wookey, O.A., *Human-Wildlife Coexistence in the Urban Domain: Promoting Welfare Through Effective Management, Responsibility and the Recognition of Mutual Interest,* in *Human/Animal Relationships in Transformation: Scientific, Moral and Legal Perspectives.* 2022, Springer. p. 317-338.

131. Sharma, P., N. Chettri, and K. Wangchuk, *Human-wildlife conflict in the roof of the world: Understanding multidimensional perspectives through a systematic review.* Ecology and evolution, 2021. **11**(17): p. 11569-11586.

132. Schell, C.J., et al., *The evolutionary consequences of human-wildlife conflict in cities.* Evolutionary Applications, 2021. **14**(1): p. 178-197.

133. Ogra, M. and R. Badola, *Compensating human-wildlife conflict in protected area communities: ground-level perspectives from Uttarakhand, India.* Human Ecology, 2008. **36**: p. 717-729.